Marchmont in Edinburgh

MALCOLM CANT

With drawings by
CLARE HEWITT

Foreword by
The Hon. JOHN R. WARRENDER, O.B.E., M.C.

JOHN DONALD PUBLISHERS LTD
EDINBURGH

to my wife
PHYLLIS

WHO ENDURED ME AND THE BOOK
FOR AS LONG AS IT TOOK

ISBN 0 85976 099 5

Reprinted 1984

Printed and bound in Great Britain by Bell & Bain Ltd., Glasgow

Foreword

Those who live in Marchmont, and many others concerned with the history of the growth and development of Edinburgh, will find much to interest them in this book. Malcolm Cant, a lifelong inhabitant of Edinburgh, has researched his facts with meticulous care and he presents them here for his readers in a clear and attractive form. His love for the district is self-evident, and his enthusiasm to share his encyclopaedic knowledge of Marchmont with his readers is infectious.

As will become clear in the text that follows, my family have been connected with parts of Marchmont since 1695. The present form of the streets and houses built on the Warrender Estates in the nineteenth century owes much to the thought and designs of my great grandfather, Sir George Warrender Bart. of Lochend, and the photographs assembled here show very clearly how much of the original Victorian townscape has survived until today. The attractive line drawings by Clare Hewitt evocatively capture and recall the atmosphere of the area before the development of Marchmont had begun.

Marchmont in Edinburgh will surely become the definitive work on the District of Marchmont and be a valuable contribution to any collection of histories of our capital city.

The Hon. John R. Warrender, O.B.E., M.C.,
Garvald,
East Lothian

Preface

In my book, *Historic South Edinburgh*, I attempted to cover a very wide field and, if I may use agricultural analogy, can claim no more than simply to have turned over a large area of ground, some of it virgin soil and much of it previously dug here and there in patches. It had been my hope that, having perhaps revealed something of the historic richness of the soil, others would have their interest stimulated and be encouraged to dig more deeply or to rake over certain parts to a finer tilth.

I am therefore delighted that my friend Malcolm Cant has produced a much more detailed study of the Marchmont district than the confines of my preliminary researches enabled me to do. I hasten to add, however, that Mr. Cant's work should not be regarded as some kind of appendix to mine. On the contrary, *Marchmont in Edinburgh* stands in its own right as a most interesting, valuable and painstaking piece of research in local history, drawn from both printed and oral sources.

The author traces the change in policy which might have created a district similar in layout and other features to the Grange, but which instead resulted in the development of one quite different but nevertheless with its own unique architectural variety and quality, and in the growth of a community with traditions and a character distinctly its own.

Marchmont is presented from its earliest and successive landowners, notably the Warrender family whose name became synonymous with the district and indeed is perpetuated in so many local street names. Here, too, is a fascinating account of events, institutions and famous residents. While many of the latter are well known and on record, it would require a world survey to trace the virtually innumerable people of distinction, especially in the professions, who, while students at the University either studiously or in graduation celebrations burned the midnight oil in their Marchmont digs. Their number must be legion, and it is to be hoped that *Marchmont in Edinburgh* will be read with interest and nostalgia by many a former if temporarily resident 'Marchmontite' now on some far distant shore – as it will be read no less widely by the local residents of today. Mr. Cant's labours and enthusiastic researches have produced a valuable contribution to the ever-continuing study of the historic riches of South Edinburgh. It is a pleasure to recommend it.

Charles J. Smith

Contents

	Page
Foreword by the Hon. John R. Warrender, O.B.E., M.C.	v
Preface by Charles J. Smith, author of *Historic South Edinburgh*	vii
Introduction	xi
1. The Feuing of Warrender Park	1
2. Marchmont	20
3. Warrender Park	34
4. Thirlestane	51
5. Spottiswoode, Arden and Lauderdale	62
6. Alvanley and Whitehouse	72
7. Strathearn and Grange	92
8. Roseneath and Argyle	114
9. The Meadows and Bruntsfield Links	135
10. Transport; Traders; People	150
Suggestions for Further Reading	172
Index	173

Introduction

The district of Marchmont has, over the years, earned itself a unique position in the hearts and minds of the people of Edinburgh, and beyond. For them and for everyone interested in the local history and architecture of the area, this short volume has been written.

It is not, of course, possible to write a book without calling upon the assistance and resources of a wide variety of people. My original inspiration undoubtedly came from reading Charles J. Smith's *Historic South Edinburgh*. When I first decided to explore the possibility of a book on the much smaller district of Marchmont, I was greatly encouraged by the interest shown by the Hon. John R. Warrender, whose family feued out the Lands of Bruntisfield in 1869. With the assistance of Mr. Douglas F. Stewart and Mrs. Angus of J. & F. Anderson, Solicitors, it soon became apparent that there was sufficient material to form the nucleus of the project. Added to that came the immense resources of the Royal Commission on the Ancient and Historical Monuments of Scotland, the Scottish Record Office, the National Library of Scotland, the Edinburgh Room of the Edinburgh Central Library, and the City Archives. Miss J. M. Barrie of New College Library and Mrs. M. N. Ramsay, Librarian to the Royal Highland Agricultural Society of Scotland, were also most helpful on particular aspects of my study. Roland A. Paxton also allowed me access to the original records of Carfrae and Belfrage, Surveyors. From the staff and members of Schools, Churches and Institutions I also received great assistance. The section and photographs dealing with St. Margaret's Convent would never have been possible without the assistance of Sister St. Ignatius. My thanks also go to the Royal Bank of Scotland and the Company of Merchants of the City of Edinburgh.

On architectural detail I was guided by the City Architect's Department, Vivienne and Stewart Tod, and Alan Marshall. On transport I constantly referred to *Edinburgh's Transport*, by D. L. G. Hunter, who courteously kept me on the right tracks. Where I dealt with street games my recollections were greatly enriched by re-reading *Golden City* and *The Singing Street* by James T. R. Ritchie.

This being an illustrated book, I was in need of constant photographic advice and expertise, which was gladly given by Malcolm Liddle. Other photographic work is credited in the book.

In addition to the photography, of course, there are the excellent line drawings by Clare Hewitt, meticulously reproducing the atmosphere of a bygone age.

The residents of Marchmont have also played their part, and it is to them that I am indebted for lending many photographs and contributing a wealth of anecdote. Sadly Mrs Loch, who showed great interest in the project, died before seeing my script in print. To my friend James Gray of the Waverley Column of the *Edinburgh Evening News* I also extend my thanks.

And finally, this book would never have been accomplished without the constant support and encouragement of my wife and family.

Malcolm Cant

CHAPTER 1

The Feuing of Warrender Park

Sir George Warrender's property at Bruntsfield was still very much a country estate in the late 1860s, but a wind of change was blowing across the green pasture land. The City of Edinburgh was beginning to move further out to the south, and already large areas of the Grange and Greenhill had been feued out by the owners, for building purposes. Entire streets of detached villas were taking shape and soon the 'Lands of Bruntisfield' would be surrounded by private development. Sir George's estate lay on well drained, gently rising ground between the Meadows on the north and the villas of the Grange on the south. The existing community was sparse. Outside the immediate environs of Bruntsfield House there were very few buildings which were not associated with the rural way of life. There were one or two quarries on the land, but they were no longer producing large quantities of stone. To the north, the Borough Loch had been drained many years previously and the Town had, at last, laid out the ground in a series of elegant pathways. Beyond the eastern boundary of Sir George's land there was a small, but thriving, community at New Campbeltown, around the area now known as Roseneath, and the Melville Drive had been laid out in 1858, giving a new sense of purpose and identity to the lands which lay to the south of the old Borough Loch.

The Bryce Feuing Plan of 1869

All these factors combined to produce a unique opportunity for the development of the Warrender estate, and Sir George soon realised its full potential. Being a man with a useful blend of integrity and business acumen, he was not long in gathering

Fig 1.   Aerial view of Marchmont and the Meadows.

Photograph by John Hudson.

together a team of experts to advise him on how best to implement his ideas. With the assistance of his solicitor, J. & F. Anderson of Edinburgh, he commissioned an architect of the highest calibre, David Bryce, and a firm of chartered surveyors, Messrs. Carfrae & Co., who had already earned themselves a very high reputation in Scotland and beyond on many contracts involving the construction of private railways, canals and other public undertakings. In deciding how best to advise Sir George, they must have been very conscious of the fact that the Warrender estate was largely self-contained, in that it was bounded to a great extent by the natural boundaries of the Meadows and Bruntsfield Links on the north and west, by St. Margaret's Convent on the south and by a row of mature trees on the east. This comparative insulation, in geographical terms, undoubtedly gave them the opportunity to develop the ground in an individual style without being inhibited by existing styles of architecture and layout.

No doubt a number of different schemes were considered, but by 1869 Carfrae had pegged out large areas of the North Park of the Warrender estate and Bryce had produced his Feuing Plan of 1869. It was an ambitious scheme in which Bryce proposed to develop the north and east sections of the estate. The main streets, running east and west, were Warrender Park Road and Warrender Park Terrace. These were linked by Marchmont Street and Spottiswoode Street, and on the eastern extremity of the estate Marchmont Crescent was formed, but not named. The position of the modern day Marchmont Road was shown, but it was named Bruntisfield Road and, of course, it did not communicate with Melville Drive because that short section of land at the north end was not within the boundary of the Warrender estate. The position and direction of the main streets followed the boundary lines, and to some extent the line, of the old hedgerows which had divided the estate into fields of crops and pasture.

When Bryce produced the feuing plan of 1869 he also submitted a series of detailed drawings for a number of elevations for the various streets. They were of an architectural

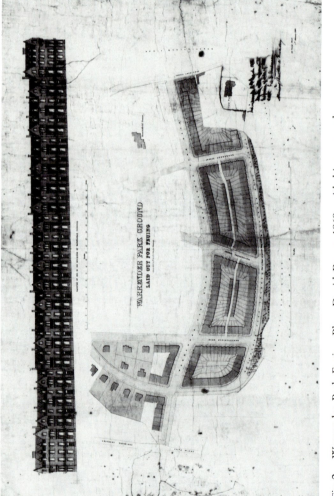

Fig 2. Warrender Park Feuing Plan: David Bryce, 1869, with his proposed elevations for Warrender Terrace.

By courtesy of the Royal Commision on the Ancient and Historical Monuments of Scotland.

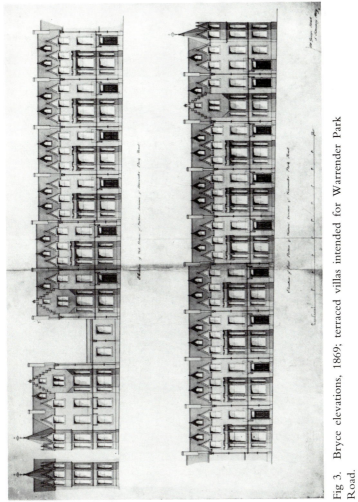

Fig 3. Bryce elevations, 1869; terraced villas intended for Warrender Park Road.

By courtesy of the Royal Commission on the Ancient and Historical Monuments of Scotland.

style strongly influenced by the Scottish Baronial idiom, but they were not tenement buildings. Whilst there is no doubt that the modern district of Marchmont is almost synonymous with the development of Scottish tenement buildings, not one of them would ever have been built if the Bryce proposals had been fully implemented. Bryce's idea was to allocate the greater part of the land to terraced villas and to use the other part, notably near the top of Marchmont Crescent, for low-density housing in the form of large detached villas. Another interesting aspect of the 1869 plan was the formation of a mews lane, entered from Bruntisfield Road, Spottiswoode Street and Marchmont Street to give access to the stables which were to be built within the rectangles formed by the terraced houses. Although the stables were never built, the plan does give an interesting insight into the social customs of the day and the class of tenant Bryce hoped to attract to his new development.

Having taken care of the lay-out of the various feus and having drawn up the appropriate plans, Bryce was then in a position to attract builders to the site. Articles and Conditions of Feu were drawn up to regulate the manner in which the work was to progress. Each feuar had to pay to Bryce a fee of two guineas to have his feu pegged out and a further fee of five guineas for a copy of the appropriate plan. Building had to be as per the feuing plan, and all the front elevations were to be of polished ashlar from Redhall or Dunmore quarries. No common stairs were permitted except on corners with the permission of the Superior, and no buildings were to be used for the sale of intoxicating liquor or for keeping gunpowder or explosives. Each feuar was entitled to sink a well and to quarry stones as he progressed, but only for use in the construction of the building, and not for re-sale. Additional burdens were placed on the feuars in Warrender Park Terrace who were required to form themselves into a Committee to regulate the use of the piece of ground opposite the building stances. They were required to fence off the area with the provision of gates at suitable points and to provide keys at 10/6d each to whoever wanted access to the ground in question. They were also under obligation to maintain the ground as an ornamental garden and to permit the building of carriage roads across it, in the event of public roads being allowed on Bruntsfield Links.

On 1st December 1869 the first feu charter was signed between Sir George Warrender and the Leith builder John Russel Swann, who opted to develop Lots 1, 2 & 3 in Marchmont Terrace. He was bound by the Articles and Conditions of Feu already referred to but he completed the houses on time and inserted the date 1870 high up on the stonework of one of the completed dwellings. Little did he know that his work was to become more significant than the circumstances justified at the time. Not only was he the first builder to put into effect the Bryce proposals, but he was also the only builder to do so. No other Bryce elevations were ever constructed, but those which were built now form that row of terraced houses in Alvanley Terrace partly occupied by the Bruntsfield Links Hotel and the Bruntsfield Park Hotel.

However, by January 1874 the main streets and drains had been laid and Bryce is recorded as having suggested 'that a portion of the ground might advantageously be laid out for a superior class of Flatted Houses instead of the self contained houses only as shown upon the plan of 1869'.

The Watherston Feuing Plan, 1876–1877

In the early part of the 1870s the Warrender estate returned to rural tranquillity and no doubt a few more harvests were brought in, in much the same way as they had been for many years previously. But Sir George had not abandoned his plans. Even if he had had moments of doubt, any businessman must have reflected long and hard after studying the Statement of Rent of Bruntisfield Park for the Year 1873:

> The whole extent of the Parks per measurement of Messrs. Carfrae & Co. in 1859 is:—

1 North Park	20.382	Acres
2 South Park	34.937	Acres
3 South West or Nunnery Park	7.675	Acres
TOTAL	62.994	
Taken off for kitchen garden since 1859	1.994	
	61.000	Acres

and the rent being £550 the average rent per acre is £9.04.

He must also have remembered that he had signed a feu charter in 1869 with John Russel Swann in which the annual feu duty per house was £19:12:0 for a piece of ground very much smaller than one acre.

Although Bryce's feuing plan had never included ground as far to the south as St. Margaret's Convent, nevertheless the Trustees of the Convent were aware in 1875 that Sir George Warrender intended to continue with his feuing arrangements and that one of the intended streets would come very close to the Convent boundary. Until a few years previously, the Convent had enjoyed absolute privacy and seclusion, being completely surrounded by farmland. Having been given first option to purchase, they hurriedly entered into an agreement with Sir George in respect of an area of approximately three acres to prevent the new development from getting too close to the Community buildings. The following year, in 1876, another Feuing Plan was announced, this time drawn up by the firm of surveyors A. Watherston & Son. This plan was in many respects quite different to that drawn up by Bryce. It was much more comprehensive in that it envisaged new streets being built on all the available land, and, in addition to that, all the proposed buildings were to be tenement buildings, of four or five storeys in height. The idea of the terraced villa, the mews lane with stables and the elegant detached houses had gone for ever. It was the plan which was to give rise to the district of Marchmont as we know it today. All the main thoroughfares were shown in their present positions with the addition of an extension to Spottiswoode Road along the line of the southern boundary of the Bruntsfield House policies, and emerging at Marchmont Terrace. All the streets were named, but present day Arden Street was named Alvanley Street and present day Alvanley Terrace was named Marchmont Terrace.

The detail in the Watherston plan of 1876 showed quite clearly that in the few years prior to its announcement considerable work had been done in laying out the position of the streets and allocating a number of building stances to well-known builders of the day. The plan certainly created great interest, with some builders applying for a single stance and others staking a claim along the entire length of one street. Among the biggest builders were W. & D. McGregor at Warrender Park Crescent; Galloway & Mackintosh at Warrender Park Road; John Pyper at Marchmont Crescent; John Souden at Marchmont Road; George Cruikshank and W.S. Cruikshank at Arden Street, Spottiswoode Street and Lauderdale Street; and Davidson & Chisholm at Thirlestane Road.

Architects of ability were also greatly in demand to draw individual elevations for each tenement, all in the Scottish Baronial style. The work attracted many eminent architects among whom were Hippolyte Blanc, John C. Hay and Edward Calvert. These were the men who designed some of Edinburgh's finest tenement buildings, described by Colin McWilliam in his book *Scottish Townscape* as having 'the large-scale splendour that can speak from a distance, with carefully composed elevations and majestic corner towers, sometimes of Baronial outline'.

A Prelude to Building

Every developer who wished to build on one of the available feus was subject to the very stringent conditions in the feu charter which required the plans for any proposed tenement to

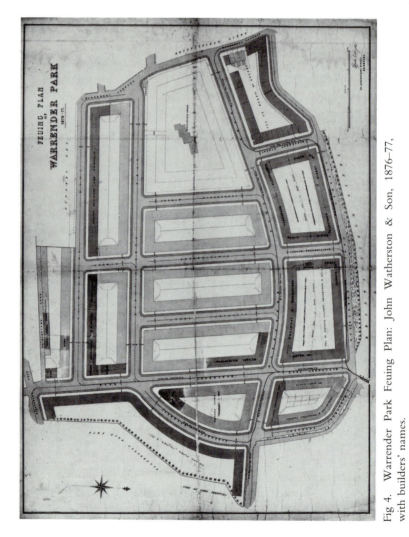

Fig 4.   Warrender Park Feuing Plan: John Watherston & Son, 1876–77, with builders' names.

By courtesy of the Royal Commission on the Ancient and Historical Monuments of Scotland.

be approved by Sir George Warrender before work was begun. In addition, the usual procedure by way of Petition to the Dean of Guild Court for permission to build was required. This latter requirement did not apply to some of the earliest tenements because it was not until 1880 that the area of authority of the Dean of Guild Court was extended to include the new district of Marchmont. This rather anomalous situation has resulted in detailed plans not being available for some of the oldest and most interesting buildings. Application to the Dean of Guild Court was certainly not a mere formality, as a number of plans were rejected and others were returned for correction or amendment. At least one eminent architect was informed that, as the proposed tenement was to be built on the site of an old quarry unknown to him, it would be necessary to submit more detailed plans showing the nature of the additional strengthening proposed for the foundations. Particular importance was also attached to the question of drainage and to ventilation of rooms which were not fitted with an outside window.

Not only was the Dean of Guild empowered to agree or disagree with the proposed plans, but he was also under a duty to hear any objection from interested parties. The Petitioner was, of course, obliged to make available full details of the plans to all persons having an interest in property which adjoined the property on which the proposed tenement was to be built. In the early days, a number of disputes arose between owners in the same tenement as to whether the owner of the top flat was permitted to develop the roof space for his own private use. Some disputes even reached the Court of Session, and in one case a long-running battle, between an existing landowner and a prospective builder, was eventually resolved by the House of Lords in favour of the builder, before the street was completed.

The attitude of the objectors to the Dean of Guild Court varied enormously. On 25.2.1884 one interested party addressed his letter to 'the Honourable the Lord Dean of Guild' and said, 'I beg to state that I do not object to said alteration but leave it entirely to your Lordship's decision believing your Lordship's decision in the matter will be perfectly safe'. That confidence in the Dean and in securing a favourable decision is not so obvious in a letter written on 17.2.1886 which stated, 'I, as owner of the adjacent property beg to protest against such shops being put up at all as they would not only be an intolerable nuisance to the whole neighbourhood but would also be detrimental to the letting of my property'.

Although the building of Marchmont was a fairly continuous process from about 1876 to 1914, it could be said that it was completed in two distinct phases which fall on either side of the year 1900. The earlier of the two phases was characterised by the individual nature of the work by builders and architects who frequently developed only one or two feus at a time. The architecture was individual in style and always in conformity with the older feu charters which required the buildings to be of the Scottish Baronial style. During this phase Warrender Park Road was built along with the streets to the north of it and also Marchmont Crescent and Marchmont Road.

In the second phase, after 1900, the individual nature of the elevations gave way to long straight facades with a somewhat monotonous continuity of style, but what they lacked in external detail was more than made up in the superior finish of the interiors. Out of the beautiful tile and mosaic stairways and landings were born the 'wally closes' of Spottiswoode Street, Spottiswoode Road, Arden Street and Lauderdale Street.

Building Work Commences

To look at the construction of a modern housing development gives us very little idea of how the masons and the joiners constructed the tenement buildings of Marchmont more than a hundred years ago. It was a mammoth building programme completed in a relatively short space of time and without any of the mechanical aids which are used in the construction industry today. But the men who built Marchmont knew their trade. The labour force was enormous and the number of wagons and horses more than Edinburgh has seen in any similar building programme since. It was as though the Victorians were making a last supreme effort to show what Scottish domestic architecture was all about. Like any building programme it reflected the mood of the age in which it was built and was designed for a way of life which has largely disappeared. Although now fully adapted to present day living, the buildings must still be considered a significant monument to the special skills of the stonemasons working at that time.

The front elevations were all constructed of good quality stone, some of which came from Edinburgh quarries and was hewn and dressed in temporary sheds on site. Some of the more specialised work on the panels, finials and other ornamentations would no doubt be done at the stonemason's yard and brought to the site when required. The feu charters actually gave permission to the builders to quarry stone from the ground on and around the place of construction. Certain limits as to depth were imposed, but all the same a considerable quantity of stone did come from the ground on which the tenements were built. The quality of the stone quarried on site would, of course, govern the use to which it was put. As each tenement was completed, there was the great tradition of inserting carved panels on the face of the buildings, depicting either the date of construction or the initials of the persons involved as architects, builders or developers.

The skill of the stonemasons on the exterior of the buildings was ably matched by the tradesmen who completed the interior of the flats. The well proportioned rooms were all finished to a very high standard of joinerwork on the doors, skirtings, and chimney pieces, in harmony with the decorative plasterwork on the ceiling roses and cornices. All the modern conveniences of the day were installed, including flush w.c.'s, baths and wash-basins, but there was no electric power. A huge black range was installed to heat the water and the oven, and to provide cooking facilities for the entire household. Town gas was installed for lighting, the ornamental brass fittings usually being hinged on long brackets which took the heat of the gas mantle away from the wall, and brought what light there was nearer to the middle of the room. Most of the principal rooms were fitted with coal burning fires; it was considered to be the height of luxury if they were used at the one time. Many of the larger flats also included maids' quarters just off the main kitchen areas and within sight and sound of the service bells which were connected to each of the main rooms of the house. Although the Victorians did not have the advantage of electric entry-phones, they did produce a system which was capable of opening the common stair door at street level, from within each of the flats or landings, and it is a credit to the standard of workmanship employed that so many of these mechanisms are still in perfect working order, after a century of use.

Carved Panels on Marchmont Tenement Buildings
(there are also innumerable single date panels)

Street	Street No.	Date	Initials	Builder/Architect
Argyle Park Terrace	2	1873	ABC	Argyle Building Company
Argyle Place	42	1875	WS	William Steele
Marchmont Crescent	1		TM	Thomas Marwick
	43		JP	John Pyper
	56		JC	John Christie
	60	1881	EC	Edward Calvert
	104	1886	JP	John Pyper
Marchmont Road	15		RM	Robert Mair
	17		JS	John Seatter
	51	1887	JP	John Pyper
	113		JCH,A	John C. Hay, Architect
	119	1880	SBC	Strathearn Building Co.
	10		EC	Edward Calvert
	124		WO	William Outerson
	144	1878	TC	Thomas Crowe
Marchmont Street	5	1882	AC	Alex Calder
Spottiswoode Street	1	1880	SH	Simon Henderson
	13	1882	SH	Simon Henderson
Thirlestane Road	58	1900	RC	Robert Chisholm
	122	1878	D.C.	Davidson & Chisholm
Warrender Park Cres.	1	1869	WDMG	W. & D. McGregor
	19		M	McGregor

Warrender Park Road	39		G&M	Galloway & Mackintosh
	77		HMI	Hugh Mackintosh
Warrender Park Terr.	3		EC	Edward Calvert
	12		CNBH	Calvert, Nisbet, Bowie and Henderson
	18	1880	JMcP	James McPherson
			EC	Edward Calvert
	21		EC	Edward Calvert
	23	1883	EC	Edward Calvert
	32A	1884	WM	William Murray
	42		GN	George Neil

The Family Names Commemorated

Like many landowners of the late nineteenth century the Warrender family had a strong affinity with their estate around Bruntsfield House, which had been under their control, continuously, since 1695. Although there were obvious advantages in feuing the ground for building purposes, there must also have been some reservations in that the family estate would never be quite the same again. Certainly the earliest feuing plan envisaged only about half of the estate being developed, but by the turn of the century the second phase of building was well under way and Bruntsfield House had ceased to be a country estate. If the fields, the cottages and the narrow country lanes were to be lost for ever, at least the family names could be carried into posterity by having them commemorated in the names of the streets under construction. The present day street names of Marchmont, Arden, Spottiswoode, Lauderdale, Thirlestane and Alvanley all relate to various Warrender family connections, particularly in and around Berwickshire, and some of the old family houses and castles are still in existence today. Although the name Bruntisfield was originally intended to be used for Marchmont Road or Warrender Park Road, the idea was later abandoned and Bruntsfield, with the slightly different spelling, now relates to that district of Edinburgh near to Marchmont but which was not built on the original 'Lands of Bruntisfield'.

Fig 5.   Carved panels: (a) Galloway & Mackintosh (Warrender Park Road); (b) Simon Henderson (Spottiswoode Street); (c) John Pyper (Marchmont Road); (d) William Outerson (Thirlestane Road).

Photographs by Hugh Fraser.

Marchmont:
>The wife of Sir George Warrender 6th Baronet was daughter to Hugh Hume Campbell of Marchmont near Greenlaw in Berwickshire.

Arden:
>From the family name of the Earl of Haddington. The 11th Earl in 1854 married Helen daughter of Sir John Warrender, by Frances, daughter of Lord Chief Justice Alvanley.

Spottiswoode:
>Hugh Hume Campbell of Marchmont married in 1834 Margaret Penelope daughter of John Spottiswoode of that Ilk.

Lauderdale:
>Sir John Warrender 5th Baronet married as his first wife in 1823 Lady Julia Maitland daughter to James 8th Earl of Lauderdale.

Thirlestane:
>Sir George Warrender's mother was daughter to the Earl of Lauderdale whose seat was Thirlestane Castle, near Lauder in Berwickshire.

Alvanley:
>The wife of Captain John Warrender was the sister of Lord Alvanley.

In addition to the names associated with the Warrender family, the modern district of Marchmont includes street names with interesting origins, chiefly associated with the other local landowners. Strathearn, with the related name Strathfillan, was derived from the Grants of Kilgraston in Strathearn, owners of the Whitehouse Estate until 1834 when it was sold to the Roman Catholic Community who founded St. Margaret's Convent. On the east side of Marchmont the name Argyle followed that of Argyle Park, a substantial villa which stood there in the early nineteenth century; and Boog Watson, the eminent authority on Edinburgh street names, suggests that neighbouring Roseneath was derived from Roseneath in Dunbartonshire, one of the seats of the Duke of Argyll. Two of the earliest and most intriguing names were Westerhall and New Campbeltown, each of which consisted of only a handful of houses in the area now known as Roseneath and Argyle.

Fig 6. Spottiswoode House, Berwickshire, latterly the property of Lady John Scott, but demolished circa 1930.

By courtesy of James Bryce.

Fig 7. Marchmont House, Berwickshire, now considerably altered.

By courtesy of James Bryce.

Fig 8.   Roseneath, Dunbartonshire, the property of the Duke of Argyll.
From an engraving by W. Wallis.

Fig 9.   Thirlestane Castle, Lauder, Berwickshire beautifully restored and now open to the public.
Courtesy of Captain the Hon. Gerald Maitland-Carew.

CHAPTER 2

Marchmont

Although Marchmont has now become the dominant name in the area, it was originally intended to refer only to individual streets within the larger district of Warrender Park. However, the transport era of the early twentieth century took Marchmont as the district name, and gradually its usage secured dominance over the family name of Warrender. What the name Warrender may have lost to the name Marchmont, by popular usage, has been more than redeemed by the fact that the name Bruntsfield is now generally used to denote an area of the city which never at any time formed part of the estate of Sir George Warrender of Bruntsfield House.

For the purpose of this chapter, Marchmont has been taken to refer only to the streets of Marchmont Crescent and Marchmont Road built near the east boundary of the estate and adjacent to the land belonging to the Dick Lauder family of Grange House.

Marchmont Crescent

The formation of the Crescent was dictated very largely by the line of the boundary between the Warrender estates and the adjacent lands. That boundary is still clearly marked by the old stone wall and trees between the lower half of Marchmont Crescent and Roseneath Place. The Crescent was shown in the earliest of the feuing plans for Warrender Park, the first of these being in 1869 by the architect David Bryce. Had Bryce's original plans been put into effect the results would have been very different to what we see today. His idea was to lay out part of the available building land in what would nowadays be described as terraced villas. The other part, notably towards the

Fig 10. Tenements in Marchmont Crescent resist bomb blast 8.10.1940.
Courtesy of Scotsman Publications Ltd.

top of the Crescent and around the area later occupied by James Gillespie's Boys' School, was to be given over to low-density housing in the form of large detached villas standing in their own private feu. The character of that part of the Crescent would therefore have been much more like the villas of Chalmers Crescent and Palmerston Road, and, of course, the School would not have been built at all. Some idea of the type of property intended can be obtained by imagining that the whole of the area now covered by the School and its playground would have been devoted to one detached house and garden.

By 1876 another feuing plan had been prepared for Sir George Warrender by the firm of Chartered Surveyors, A. Watherston & Son of Edinburgh. Again Marchmont Crescent was shown and named but the feuing stances were arranged

c

for the construction of tenement buildings. It was the feuing plan of 1876 which was to give birth to the Crescent as we know it today. Work began at the north end about 1877, but the last tenement at the south end was not completed until about 1886. In that decade Marchmont saw a great influx of architects and masons keen to put their stamp on the building project of the day. They built five-storey tenements at the north end and later four-storey tenements at the south end, that section being known as Marchmont Crescent South. Although all reference to 'South' was discontinued as early as 1882, it could be said, for example, that the address 39 Marchmont Crescent in 1982 would have been 18 Marchmont Crescent South in 1882.

Today the line of the Crescent and the style of the architecture show very little variation from the original. A number of interesting carved panels can be seen depicting either the date of construction of the tenement or the initials of the architect or builder. Several houses in and around the Crescent were built by John Pyper, whose descendants still live in Edinburgh, as well as in Newcastle upon Tyne. In a street which abounds in architectural interest it is difficult to be selective without running the risk of omitting some special feature which ought to be mentioned. There is no doubt, however, that no one could visit Marchmont without noticing the tenement building at the corner of Marchmont Crescent and Marchmont Road. The architect and the builder obviously decided that this was to be the show piece of the area, built as it is on a naturally commanding position overlooking the Meadows. The building presents a most ornate broad gable supporting a stone balcony and flanked by twin corbelled turrets of Scottish Baronial style. There are tiny windows near roof level and the whole building is topped by a sitting lion, caressing a shield. It was built in 1878 by Galloway and Mackintosh and probably designed by Thomas P. Marwick, the initials T.M. appearing within the circled pediment of the highest window. For many years now the spacious ground-floor accommodation has been occupied by the long-established business of Arnold Seftor Ltd., the furrier.

Fig 11. Horse power, old and new, compete in Marchmont Crescent.
Courtesy of Scotsman Publications Ltd.

When the Crescent was being laid out, great emphasis was placed on the design of the corner blocks, which frequently displayed a great number of architectural features. The house at No. 21 on the corner with Warrender Park Road was certainly no exception to this rule, designed with a basement flat, a massive rounded spire at roof level, and an interesting corbelled turret built from the edge of the angle elevation. It was built around 1878 for National Heritages Association Ltd., but by 1881 the Company had come to the conclusion that this vast flat could be conveniently and profitably divided into two separate dwellings. Observant Marchmont people will already have noticed the telltale signs. Close examination of No. 21 reveals that the left-hand window was at one time the door and the rather curious narrow window on the right is all that remains of the much larger original window. Round the corner is the entrance to the second dwelling, now 23 Warrender Park Road. The darker facing stones to the left-hand side of the entrance to No. 23 show that it was a window in the original building.

Although there is little doubt that the dominant style of architecture in the Crescent is Scottish Baronial, one architect, Thornton Shiells, contributed a striking contrast to the work done by other architects. His design for Nos. 32–42 is completely devoid of crowsteps, corbels or turrets but has a distinctive, almost Gothic, appearance about it. The strong perpendicular lines of the bay windows and the absence of string courses above the first-floor level give it an identity distinct from the horizontal lines of the adjacent buildings. The roofline stonework is most intricate, displaying elegant finials and ornate clam-shells.

Fortunately much of the architecture remains intact to this day, although a century of wind and rain has taken its toll among some of the more intricate work, and particularly on the vulnerable chimney heads, many of which have been shortened to effect a more economic repair.

Warrender Park Board School: James Gillespie's Boys' School

In 1882, although Marchmont Crescent South was only partially completed, the Edinburgh School Board had already acquired the site at the junction with Marchmont Road, and they had commissioned the Board's architect Robert Wilson to draw up the necessary plans to erect a public school under the authority of the Education (Scotland) Act 1872. The decision to build the school on that site was criticised on the grounds that the type of house in the district was intended for persons who were unlikely to send their children to a Board school. However, it was hoped that this opposition would gradually die out and that the residents would be happy to take advantage of the school's new facilities for their children. In support of the decision to place the school in the new district of Marchmont one report stated 'that so far as the buildings

Fig 12. Warrender Park Board School, *circa* 1900.
Courtesy of W.B. Grubb.

are concerned the school is far in advance of the generality of
private adventure schools most of which are located in
buildings intended to be occupied as dwelling houses, the
ventilation and accessories of which must necessarily be
insufficient for the use of a large number of scholars'.

It was against this social background that the Warrender
Park School began its long history in the service of education.
Reference to the Edinburgh School Board Directory indicates
that it was not long in overcoming any initial difficulties,
because by 1889 the average attendance (boys and girls) was
880 and a full range of subjects was taught. The School was
divided into a Juvenile Department under the Headmaster
James Andrew and an Infant Department under the
Headmistress Annie Gibson. In addition to the standard and
class subjects the curriculum included domestic economy,
French, German, gymnastics and callisthenics, Latin,
mathematics, religious knowledge, singing, and special
instruction to pupil teachers, of whom there were twelve
associated with the school. The music department was in the

capable hands of James Sneddon, Mus.Bac.(Cantab). In 1882, long before the European Court had anything to say about corporal punishment in Scottish schools, the Edinburgh School Board stated 'that the Board is very desirous that, as far as possible, the infliction of corporal punishment should be avoided during the time set apart for Religious Instruction'.

By the year 1889 the school fees ranged from 1/- for every four weeks, at infant level, up to 3/4d every four weeks for the most senior class, and the headmaster's salary was £420 per annum out of a total expenditure for the year of £2538: 1: 5.

From its earliest beginnings there was a system of pupil-teachers at Warrender Park which gave certain young ladies the opportunity of practical training as teachers in the school in which they had been pupils. Two of the girls concerned had reason to be proud of their involvement in the new district of Marchmont. When Ann Christie left her father's house in the morning at 36 Marchmont Crescent to walk the short distance to the school, she would pass a number of the most interesting tenements built by her father, John Christie, just a few years previously. The other young lady was Helen Budge, whose father John Budge built sections of Marchmont Road to the south of the school.

The passage of time eventually clouds all memory, but perhaps never more so than when grandfathers are recalling the disciplined nature of their schooldays and their rigorous training in the three R's. For some, the realisation that in fact only one of the three hallowed subjects commences with the letter R may well find its explanation in the standard of general education which was actually in existence at the time of a class report in 1886 when the inspector said that the class 'showed a marked disposition to be restless, inattentive and talkative—intelligence decidedly weak—extremely defective in history and geography with papers disfigured by bad spelling'. The same inspector must also have struck a disconsolate note in the ear of James Sneddon when he said that the general effect of the class singing was marred by an omission to isolate those children who had no ear for music!

Fig 13. Warrender Park School Medallion presented to Margaret Brown, 1895.

Courtesy of Mrs. E. Smith.

A later generation of pupils must have been in much higher spirits when the headmaster announced a holiday on 24.6.1914 to celebrate the 600th anniversary of the Battle of Bannockburn, but it is doubtful if any of the youngsters gave much thought to what lay ahead in the field of conflict. By October 1914 the school building had been requisitioned by the War Office and the children were transferred to Sciennes School where their education was continued under the rather unsatisfactory double shift system. The headmaster, in a rather sombre mood, recorded in his daily log that one of his most promising young masters, Matthew Higgins, M.A., left the school to enlist in Lord Kitchener's Army.

When the school re-opened for the autumn term in 1923 it was to enter into a new chapter in its history, now under the name James Gillespie's Junior School. By 1929, following the decision of the Education Committee to restrict entry to girls only at the Bruntsfield Links school building, the Marchmont Crescent school building was used for boys only with a commencing enrolment of 432. Within the first decade, however, the country and the school were thrown into confusion yet again in the months which led up to the Second World War. Part of the school was taken over by the Military, with the ground floor being used for storing and assembling gas masks, and fire drills became ever more frequent until the pupils could evacuate the building in just over one minute. In May 1939 the A.R.P. officials were very much in evidence, distributing labels and notices for possible evacuation of all children. As the anxiety grew, a trial evacuation was run on 28.8.1939, with a party leaving the school at 9.30 a.m. to walk to the rendezvous point at Blackford Hill Station. Within days the political situation had worsened and a full evacuation was ordered, 106 pupils being hurriedly moved out to Blackford Hill Station en route for Gordon and Nenthorn. The pupils who remained in Edinburgh were taught in private houses in various parts of Marchmont.

At the end of the Second World War the school settled down once more to concentrate on the education of young boys from every part of Edinburgh, in an era dominated by a number of very able headmasters. Whilst it was always regretted by parents that there was no Secondary Department to match that of James Gillespie's High School for Girls, nevertheless the Boys' School did continue for many years to produce a high ratio of entrants to George Heriot's School, the

Fig 14. James Gillespie's Boys' School—Craigour Championship, with Andy Irvine (centre row first from left).
Courtesy of W.B. Grubb.

Merchant Company Schools, the Royal High School and Boroughmuir School. Following further reorganisation the school closed in 1973 when its function was incorporated in the new James Gillespie's Primary School within the Bruntsfield House complex. The last headmaster, Harold S. Wall, M.A., closed the school log on 10.9.1973.

Marchmont Road

The development of Marchmont Road was in many ways similar to that of the Crescent. It was always intended to be one of the main thoroughfares of the district, running almost directly south from the Meadows up to the traffic lights at Strathearn Road. The position of the road was shown in

Fig 15. Gillespie Old Boys: (a) Andy Irvine, Scottish Rugby Captain; (b) Ronnie Corbett, Television Personality; (c) Alastair Sim, Actor; (d) David Steel, Politician.

Fig 15c by courtesy of Scotsman Publications Ltd.

Bryce's drawing of 1869, but it was referred to as Bruntisfield Road and, like the Crescent, was intended to have detached villas around the area close to James Gillespie's Boys' School. The remainder of the housing was to have been terraced villas to a uniform design prepared by Bryce himself. One of the interesting features of the 1869 plan was that access to a mews lane was intended about the middle of the north-west section, i.e. about the position now occupied by No. 10 Marchmont Road. The lane would have given access to rows of stables and coachhouses built partly on the area now used as back greens. However, the Bryce plans were never put into effect.

By 1876 the Watherston plan had been drawn up showing Marchmont Road laid out for tenement development with some of the more prominent feus already taken by well-known builders of the day. The first of the tenements began to appear about 1878, Galloway & Mackintosh operating at the north end and Thomas Crowe operating at the south and close to Thirlestane Lane. Within ten years, and with the assistance of a great number of other builders and architects, most of the available land had been built on and the houses let to prospective tenants. The last section to be completed was between Spottiswoode Road and Warrender Park Road. Before this was done, there was still considerable evidence of open countryside because nothing had been built between the west side of Marchmont Road and Bruntsfield House. The area now occupied by Arden Street, Spottiswoode Street and Lauderdale Street was still under pasture and the animals were prevented from straying by an old stone wall which ran down about the line of the west pavement in Marchmont Road. This wall was referred to and shown in plans prepared by an architect as late as 1888 but was swept away a few years later when his plans were put into effect.

The road is rich in architectural detail of the Scottish Baronial style, much of it remaining unaltered to the present day. This style of architecture was certainly very much in the minds of Edward Calvert and Alex Macnaughten when they drew up plans for the section of the road between Warrender

Fig 16. Shops now occupy the original main-door flat at No. 27, Marchmont Road.

Photograph by A.C. Robson.

Park Terrace and Warrender Park Road. Even the quality and colour of the stone lends itself to the overall effect and the individual detail is intriguing. There are mock gargoyles, obscure panels, spiked targes, castellated chimney breasts and rope string courses. Within the conventional stonework at roof level of Nos. 14 and 16 there is a reminder of conventional warfare of an earlier century. Two cannons, formed out of stone, stand sentinel against attack from the east. At No. 6 there is also a shield formed within the recess of the overhanging stonework, and although at first glance the inscription appears very obscure, it does, in fact, contain nothing more than the date 1879 written in a peculiar slanting style very characteristic of some of Calvert's other work. He added his signature with the initials E.C. above No. 10.

Many eminent architects were involved in drawing elevations for Marchmont tenements, but perhaps the most eminent of all was Hippolyte Blanc, who earned himself the reputation of an architect of very diverse talents. In addition to restoring the Great Hall at Edinburgh Castle he was responsible for the design of a number of Edinburgh churches, notably Cluny Parish Church (formerly St. Matthew's). Unfortunately, much of the detail which he intended for Nos. 21–25 was omitted when the building was completed in 1880, but his involvement does illustrate the calibre of the architects involved at that time.

At the top end of the road, on the east side, an equally eminent builder was making his mark around the same time. John Souden, who was later involved in the construction of the new *Scotsman* building on the North Bridge, also headed a consortium of builders and traders under the name of Strathearn Building Company. In 1880 they started building up near Beaufort Road and worked down year by year to meet up with work done by Palmerston Building Association in 1884. At No. 113 there is a panel JCH,A referring to John C. Hay, the Architect, and higher up on the same building the mason has left the characteristic sign of the rule and the square. Another interesting feature of the building is the very narrow window to the side of the main door entrances. In the original plan of 1880 the architect Mr. Hay made a special feature of this window which was to provide natural light to the 'piano recess' formed just off the parlour. Had the architect only known that Marchmont was to earn the nickname 'kippers and pianos', he might also have included in the kitchen plan some special reference to the preparation of that essentially Scottish tea!

CHAPTER 3

Warrender Park

At the end of the nineteenth century there still existed the practice of including in the designation of place names the word 'Park', rather reminiscent of the rural nature of the open countryside. There was Greenhill Park, Hope Park and the new and growing district of Warrender Park, which was the name given to the district of Marchmont as we now know it. When David Bryce the architect was laying out the street plans for Warrender Park Road and Warrender Park Terrace, he was so confident about the suitability of the site that he told his prospective developers that the district only required to be known to be appreciated. On the other hand, more than one hundred years later and against a background of growing social change *Student* magazine for October 1981 described the character of Warrender Park Road/Street, Avenue, Crescent, By-Pass as sadly epitomising the dreariest aspects of student life in the 1980s. Whatever be the truth between these two conflicting opinions, it is certainly true to say that when Bryce drew up his plans he could not have had any insight into the social requirements of today, any more than we can estimate the social requirements for the year 2080. In any case, he can rest peacefully: his plans were never implemented.

As with many of the older parts of Marchmont, the original intention was to build terraced villas to a uniform design along the entire length of Warrender Park Terrace from Marchmont Road at the east end to Marchmont Street at the west end. However, after the Bryce proposals had been abandoned, a group of men from very different backgrounds came together in 1878 to form a consortium for the development of what was described as the Eastern Division of Warrender Terrace. They were Simon Henderson a master baker, John Nisbet a hotelier, John Bowie a doctor of medicine, and Edward

Calvert an architect. No doubt Messrs. Henderson, Nisbet and Bowie were involved in a financial capacity, but it was Edward Calvert who was most involved in the practicalities of the project. He was a young ambitious architect from Hull who married the daughter of an established builder, and later moved to Edinburgh where he developed a passion for the Scottish Baronial style so prevalent at that time. He drew plans for the entire section of the Eastern Division and was responsible for annotating his work with a number of interesting carved panels on the face of the buildings depicting the years of construction 1878–1883 and the initials of himself and the other petitioners. The *esprit de corps* of the consortium was carried into posterity by the panel above No. 12 containing the surname initials H.N.B.C. Calvert lived for a while in No. 8 at a time when he was building up a successful practice in Edinburgh.

Two other houses in the Terrace deserve notice, both of which are owned by the University of Edinburgh. No. 17 is Stirling-Maxwell House and No. 19 is Fleming House, the names being those of past Rectors of the University.

Sir William Stirling-Maxwell, Spanish scholar, historian and virtuoso, was born in 1818 at Kenmure, the only son of Archibald Stirling of Keir. In 1865, on the death of his uncle, Sir John Maxwell, he succeeded to the Baronetcy and assumed the additional name of Maxwell. A few years later he took an active part in organising an exhibition in Edinburgh of pictures and manuscripts concerning Sir Walter Scott, and in the following year, 1872, he was installed as Rector of Edinburgh University.

The other worthy gentleman was Sir Alexander Fleming, born on 6.8.1881 at Lochfield near Darvel and known the world over for his discovery of penicillin. In John Malkin's biography of Fleming there are listed seven pages of Honours bestowed upon this great man, one of which, in 1951, was Lord Rector of Edinburgh University.

The Western Division of Warrender Park Terrace was completed between 1880 and 1884, Mr. Thomas Marwick the architect making a special feature of the entrance doorways by including the knotted rope design similar to that which can be seen on the main entrance to St. Margaret's Convent in Whitehouse Loan. Many of the architects and builders who were involved in the construction of Warrender Park Terrace also did work around the same time in the lower part of Spottiswoode Street and the east side of Marchmont Street.

Royal Highland & Agricultural Society of Scotland

There are few people in Edinburgh who do not know Ingliston, situated just to the west of the City, which in recent years has become a centre for a variety of recreational pastimes. Since 1960 Ingliston has also been the permanent site of the annual show of the Royal Highland and Agricultural Society of Scotland, first established in 1784. Before 1960 the Society favoured the idea of the 'Show Circuit', choosing a different location each year, in various parts of the country. Whilst the system was undoubtedly popular in that it brought the Show much nearer to the farming community of Scotland, eventually rising costs and other disadvantages were such that the Society decided on a permanent showground. After careful consideration, Ingliston was chosen, the site being close to Edinburgh Airport and the motorways of central Scotland. There were, of course, a number of interesting shows before the days of Ingliston.

During the summer of 1842 Edinburgh prepared itself to play host to the Society's 'great cattle show' widely advertised in the Scottish newspapers of the day. It was not, of course, just a cattle show because it included a great variety of livestock, implements of husbandry, seeds, and produce. The site chosen was eight acres of the North Park of Sir George Warrender's land between what is now Warrender Park Terrace and Warrender Park Road. It was considered as an ideal site closed in by a range of fine old trees and formed on four sides of a rectangle by stands for horses and cattle.

Towards the centre of the arena pens were constructed for sheep and pigs, and on the north side (close to the boundary with Bruntsfield Links) there was a large tent for the exhibition of roots, seeds, grains, dairy produce and wool. On the south side and commanding a unique view of the entire show was the gallery for the ladies, constructed on top of the apartments laid aside for the use of the judges and the committee. In front of the gallery was a stage for the presentation of prizes to the winners of the various competitions.

Altogether, it was a familiar scene to the farming community of Scotland who had travelled long distances to be present at the great annual event. As with any major national event, special arrangements were made to cope with the pressure on normal travelling facilities. With characteristic Scottish reserve, the entrepreneurs of the day rose to the occasion—by providing two extra coaches, one leaving Mrs. Hay's Inn, Hawick at 6 a.m. and the other leaving the Bridge Inn, Galashiels at 7 a.m. By all accounts the Show was a great success, it being recorded that 5,000 people were waiting at five o'clock in the morning at the entrance gate just to see the animals going in and being allocated to the appropriate stands. As the day wore on, so great was the attendance that the people spilled over onto Bruntsfield Links, which was utilised for setting out tables and chairs for the supply of all kinds of viands.

To mark the occasion there was also an open-air concert and a fireworks display at Warriston Park and a ball for the ladies and gentlemen at the Assembly Rooms in George Street.

Some years later in 1859 the Society returned to the Warrender estate when a much bigger area of ground was laid out for a much enlarged show. In addition to the usual array of farm livestock, mechanisation was beginning to show its effects with the use of steam-driven machinery. One of the chief items, manufactured by Burgess & Kay of London and exhibited by James Shaw of Ayton, was McCormack's reaper, which stood alongside a range of more humble implements

D

such as turnip cutters, root washers, churns and cheese presses. There were leisure corners also. In what must have been the 'ideal homes exhibition' of 1859 J.T. Alexander of Carnoustie displayed tasteful and fancy summerhouses for gardens or pleasure grounds, and a variety of elaborate drinking fountains. In these days, of course, not only was a woman's work never done but it was never easy either, at least not without Thomas Bradford's patent washing, wringing and mangling machine which claimed to be capable of dealing with an 80 lb load of linen. The machine consisted of a large watertight box hung on its axis and capable of an oscillating movement so that the clothes were thrown against the wooden ribs on the inside of the box. Apparently the Prince of Wales was so taken with it that he dismounted from his horse to examine its mechanical arrangement at closer range, but it is not recorded what the ladies thought of it.

A feature of the 1859 show was the reaping and grass-cutting competition which took place at Myreside Farm a few miles to the west of the main showground. A large crowd attended on a very hot afternoon to see all the latest machinery powered by portable steam engines. The nobility included the Duke of Atholl and Sir Hugh Hume Campbell, Bart., and one of the judges was George Bertram of Sciennes.

Viewpark

Many years before Sir George Warrender feued out his land for building purposes, the Warrender family had acquired a number of smaller estates in the vicinity of Bruntsfield House. One of these estates was Brown's Acres on which stood the property later known as Viewpark. In the 1870s Viewpark was still a substantial two-storey building with an elegant square tower, commanding a unique position at the head of Bruntsfield Links. It may well have remained like that for many more years but for the decision to feu the 'Lands of Bruntisfield'.

Fig 17.   Viewpark School in Warrender Park Crescent, demolished 1900.
Photograph courtesy of Miss Wilma Gladstone.

As early as 1869, when the first of the Bryce buildings were being erected in Alvanley Terrace, certain stipulations were made for the protection of Viewpark's amenity. In these days, the boundary wall came within ten feet of the house now occupied as an hotel in Alvanley Terrace. But shortly after the Watherston Feuing Plan was announced in 1876, a large part of the garden ground belonging to Viewpark was sold to permit the building of Warrender Park Crescent. The tenement buildings were completed in 1881, by which time the east section of Viewpark had been acquired as a school, and an elegant studio in the Grecian style of architecture had been built in the south-west corner of the grounds. This studio was first used by George Shaw the photographer and portrait painter before being taken over by Andrew Swan Watson, the well-known Edinburgh photographer.

In the years which followed, Viewpark saw many more changes. At the turn of the century it became the centre of attention again as proposals for the demolition and

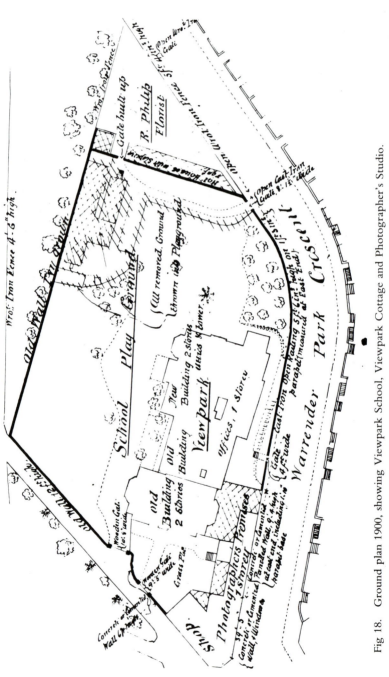

Fig 18.   Ground plan 1900, showing Viewpark School, Viewpark Cottage and Photographer's Studio.

Courtesy of J. & F. Anderson, Solicitors

development of the site were put before the Dean of Guild Court. It was a prime site, and there was a great deal of public interest in preserving the amenity of an area so close to Bruntsfield Links. A lively exchange of views in the *Edinburgh Evening Dispatch* in March 1901 revealed that the Viewpark grounds had been considered as a possible site for the Usher Hall, but it was not that proposal which incurred the wrath of the adjacent property owners. In the 1870s the secluded privacy of Viewpark had been rudely disturbed by the building of Warrender Park Crescent. But since then the owners of the tenement flats had become used to towering above the grounds of Viewpark, and they were unhappy at the prospect of losing their supremacy, particularly when they learned that the proposal was to build more tenements on the other side of the street and at a feu duty much lower than that prevailing in neighbouring properties. By a cruel irony, Viewpark was set for revenge! Fortunately for the existing property owners the Dean of Guild Court had already come to the conclusion that a number of improvements to the plans would be required, and the builder decided, in the face of mounting opposition, to abandon his application.

Boroughmuir School: James Gillespie's School

There has been some form of educational establishment on the Viewpark site for at least a hundred years. The original Villa was occupied as Viewpark School as early as 1881 under the headmastership of William Donaldson, M.A., but the school was demolished around 1901 in the ill-fated attempt by W.S. Cruikshank to build tenement properties on the site. In a report to the Dean of Guild Court in 1901 it was said that the site was a commanding and important piece of ground seen from all sides and that the proposed method of laying it out was not commendable from a public point of view.

After the idea of using the site for the Usher Hall had been abandoned, progress was made in building the much needed

Fig 19.   Dux Medal, 1910–11, awarded to Susan H. Newlands, lies unclaimed at Boroughmuir High School.

Courtesy of Boroughmuir High School

Boroughmuir School, which was opened in September 1904. Although classes were begun in September, the formal opening by the Right Hon. Charles Scott Dickson, K.C., M.P., Lord Advocate, was delayed until 3.2.1905. After his tour of the school the Lord Advocate stated that 'the most striking characteristic of every class is the high and perfectly uniform level of proficiency'. Against a background like that it was obviously not long before the school began building up various organisations and its involvement in sport. Although the school went on to achieve pre-eminence on the rugby field, there was also great involvement in football, hockey, tennis and golf. A great feature of the sports calendar was the taking of the annual team photographs in the garden of Swan Watson's Studio just next to the school. However, within a very short time of its being opened, the Edinburgh School Board discovered that the intake of pupils was very much greater than had been anticipated and that a new site was required. In 1909 the Board made an approach to the Trustees of St. Margaret's Convent in Whitehouse Loan to purchase part of the Convent grounds fronting Thirlestane Road for the purpose of building a school. Whilst the site may well have been most suitable, it was discovered that the legal restrictions on the use of the ground prevented its being used for a school. Undeterred, the Board continued its search and eventually decided on the Viewforth site where the new Boroughmuir was opened in 1914.

When Boroughmuir vacated their old building in 1914, the School Board arranged for extensive internal alterations to be made before James Gillespie's School transferred from the old Gillespie's Hospital building in Gillespie Crescent. In its early days at Bruntsfield Links, James Gillespie's was co-educational, but in 1929 the Education Committee decided to restrict intake to girls only, thereby laying the foundation for a school which for many years was to operate as James Gillespie's High School for Girls. In 1933 the last link with Viewpark disappeared when the old Viewpark Cottage and Swan Watson's Studio were demolished to make way for an annexe to house the growing population of Gillespie girls. Of all the eminent headmistresses associated with the School, Miss May Andrew, C.B.E., M.A., will be remembered most of all by pupils and teachers alike.

In recent years the building was re-occupied as part of Boroughmuir School after the new James Gillespie's School was built in the grounds of Bruntsfield House (see Chapter 6).

Fig 20. Warrender Park Crescent has retained its quiet residential appearance for more than 100 years.

Photograph by A.C. Robson

Warrender Park Road

Warrender Park Road, or Bruntisfield Road as it was first called, was intended to be the main thoroughfare through the new district of Warrender Park, providing communication between Whitehouse Loan in the west and the area now known as Sciennes in the east. In the early days Marchmont Road did not communicate with Melville Drive and, in any case, there was very little traffic running north and south through the district. Warrender Park Road was therefore built as a wide gracious thoroughfare which, in the course of its construction, attracted a wide range of builders and architects. After the Bryce proposals had been abandoned, building work commenced at the east end shortly after the Watherston Feuing Plan had been announced in 1876. At the west end the elegant buildings overlooking the Bruntsfield House policies were constructed as part of W. & D. McGregor's plans which were

Fig 21. Warrender Park Road, with the Usher Institute, 1911.

Fig 22. Queen Mary, just discernible beneath the floral headgear, in Warrender Park Road, 1911.

Courtesy of John Horberry & Son

completed between 1878 and 1881. This was the era of the small building association, usually made up of the master joiners and masons who actually worked on the buildings. There was the Park Road Building Association at No. 123, the Marchmont Building Association at No. 135, the Mutual Building Association at No. 103, the Brownisfield Building Association at No. 115 and—perhaps most colourful of all— Saint Gillie Grange Building Association at No. 99. The whole of the north section between Marchmont Road and Spottiswoode Street was built by Galloway & Mackintosh, the initials G & M appearing near the Marchmont Road end where the work was started in 1881, and the initials of Mackintosh only appearing near the Spottiswoode Street end, when the work was completed in 1883.

Apart from the tenements of Warrender Park Road there are, or were, two buildings which deserve special mention in view of their undoubted contribution to the welfare of the citizens of Edinburgh, both in body and spirit. The building which still exists is the John Usher Institute of Public Health, and the other building was the original Warrender Park Free Church.

The Usher Institute

In the pursuit of local history there is always a temptation to dwell on 'the good old days' by contrast with what is bad in present-day society and to yearn for the slower, more relaxed way of life of former times. In doing this, we tend to ignore the enormous advances which have been made in medical science and which were totally non-existent in what would be more accurately described as 'the bad old days'.

In the mid-nineteenth century one man, Professor William P. Alison, was acutely aware of the state of the nation's health and resolved, with others, to do something about it. Although he was forced into premature retirement by ill-health in 1856, he was fortunate to see his ideas taken up and advanced by

Henry Littlejohn, who became the Medical Officer of Health for Edinburgh in 1862. During Littlejohn's term of office, diseases like cholera and typhus gradually disappeared from Edinburgh houses, and it was he who was instrumental in getting the Town Council to secure a special Act of Parliament compelling the notification of cases of infectious diseases. By the 1880s the study of bacteriology, in the wake of Pasteur, had given medicine a new confidence and sense of purpose. This was very much in the mind of Alexander Low Bruce when he was introduced to Pasteur at the time of the Edinburgh University tercentenary celebrations in 1884, as a result of which Bruce resolved to fulfil his ambition to found a new chair of Public Health in Edinburgh. Although he did not live to see his dream come true, he left specific instructions with his legal adviser as to how his bequest was to be used. Donations were gathered from a wide variety of sources, and with the assistance of Sir John Usher of Norton a sum of £15,000 was made available for the establishment of a chair of Public Health in 1898. Four years later the generosity of Sir John Usher provided sufficient funds for the building of related laboratories. In his deed of gift Sir John Usher stated:

> In the year one thousand eight hundred and ninety eight I made an offer to the University Court of the University of Edinburgh to the effect that as soon as a Chair of Public Health should have been established in that University and a Professor appointed I would build and equip a laboratory and classroom to be used exclusively for the teaching of Public Health in connection with the Chair of Public Health on condition that the site of that proposed new building should be provided by the University and that the building should be called 'The John Usher Institute of Public Health' at the same time expressing the wish that the said Institute should be made useful to the Public Health Administration of the City of Edinburgh.

A site was secured in Warrender Park Road, plans were drawn by the architects Leadbetter & Fairley, and the new John Usher Institute of Public Health came into being in 1902. As though in awe and wonder at the work being done within its portals, the Highway Department of the day arranged for wooden setts instead of granite setts to be placed in the roadway outside, so that the concentration of the students in the lecture hall would not be broken by the sound of wagon wheels rumbling past outside.

Since its inauguration in 1902 the Institute has been served by a long line of eminent professors and has in turn served the community through the ages in many different ways. In the early days under Professor Stewart the groundwork was done in establishing the laboratory and building up the degree courses for the students. Later generations made significant changes brought about partly by the advances in medical science and partly by changes in emphasis regarding the function of the Institute *vis-à-vis* other departments of the University. A new one-year Diploma in Public Health was introduced by Professor Lelean after his appointment in 1926.

The Institute was not without its colourful characters. Mr. Bott, a technician, was gratefully remembered by generations of students to whom he offered the invaluable extra-curricular facility of 'Bott's Swotts'—'for a modest sum he was prepared to show groups of undergraduates those of the Professor's slides which he thought were most likely to feature in the final examination'.

The story of the Usher Institute and of the evolution of community medicine in Edinburgh was written in 1975 by Dr. Una Maclean, giving a very lucid and comprehensive review of the work of the Institute from its earliest beginnings.

Warrender Park Free Church

In the early 1880s the population of Marchmont was increasing at a great pace. Many of the tenement buildings had been completed, allowing families and domestic staff to move in, and shopkeepers were busy setting up what they hoped would be successful businesses. In these days, perhaps more so than nowadays, the Church played an important part in establishing

Fig 23.   Warrender Park Free Church (the Iron Church) from a line drawing by Clare Hewitt.

and maintaining community life. Within a little more than a stone's throw there was the old-established Barclay Free Church, but it was having difficulty in accommodating all the people from Warrender Park who wished to attend. The Church was not slow to respond to the problem. In November 1882 a decision was taken by the Free Church Presbytery to form a new congregation at Warrender Park, and until a suitable site was found, Sunday services were conducted in Viewpark School in Warrender Park Crescent.

But there remained the problem of finding a permanent site, which was not made easier by the fact that values and feu-duties were high. However, the district was by no means completely built up, and although the north side of Warrender Park Road was residential, the south side had a very rural air about it. In fact, at times, perhaps the air was more than rural because in a field just at the bottom of what is now Lauderdale Street the Glasgow firm of cattle dealers McQuade & Nelson kept a herd of mobile bullocks. If the Warrender Park Free Mission Station was going to shift a herd of bullocks, their

committee would require to carry some weight! Good men
were not in short supply. A committee of eight was formed
which included two clergymen, a chartered accountant, a
solicitor and a group of men whose names were to become
household words in Edinburgh. There was Henry Blyth the
draper of Earl Grey Street, William Brown the bookseller of
Princes Street, William Turnbull the auctioneer of George
Street, and David Wishart the iron merchant of Picardy Place.

The site was secured from Sir George Warrender on a five-
year lease, plans were drawn up by the architect D.A.
Robertson, and an iron church was erected in 1885. One of
the conditions of the lease was that the committee were to be
liable in event of any damage being done to the livestock, but
no incident was ever reported. The congregation grew in
strength and influence, adding two modest transepts to the
church in 1890. Under one of its first ministers, Rev. Thomas
Currie, the church made great progress in associating itself
with the special needs of the immediate district. From the
earliest days there was a Young Women's Meeting at 5 p.m.
every Sunday afternoon at which the domestic servants of the
district met for tea and religious instruction. Open-air services
were held on Bruntsfield Links, and there was a special
involvement with the student population which has been a
feature of Marchmont since it was built. Under the direction
of Rev. Thomas Currie it soon became evident that the Iron
Church could only be regarded as temporary accommodation.
The Church Extension Committee had already negotiated with
Sir George Warrender to take first refusal of the site at the
corner of Warrender Park Road and Spottiswoode Street, but
they did not take up the offer, and instead the site was taken
for the John Usher Institute of Public Health.

By 1890 the congregation had taken the decision to build a
new stone church in Whitehouse Loan, the foundation stone
being laid on 23.5.1891. The Iron Church was kept as an
annexe for a number of years but was eventually disposed of in
1897.

CHAPTER 4

Thirlestane

Built on the southern edge of the Warrender estate, the streets of Thirlestane offer yet another contrast in a district dominated by tenement development. It was here that some of the earliest buildings were erected at a time when feelings were running high between the tenant farmers of the South Park and the speculative builders of Marchmont. Here, too, the district saw fulfilled one of the early ideas of providing mews lanes for stables and coachmen's houses, but the owners had taken up residence in the Grange nearby.

Thirlestane Road

Although Thirlestane Road lacks the architectural interest of some of the other streets nearby, nevertheless it is a broad, well-proportioned street with a number of very elegant flats. The unusual thing about Thirlestane Road is that although the elevations are almost identical to one another, much of it was designed and constructed by the same men who produced much more intricate work in Marchmont Road, nearby. What is more, although the plain frontages give the impression of having been built in more modern times, many of them were commenced as early as 1878. Mr. Bryce, the architect, did not include Thirlestane Road in his feuing plan of 1869, and therefore there is no record of any Bryce elevations for this street. It was, however, shown in Watherston's feuing plan of 1876 with all the feus on the north side already allocated. Strangely, only one feu was allocated on the south side, which was developed in 1878 as Nos. 13, 15, 17. The opposite side of the road between Marchmont Road and Spottiswoode Street was built by a variety of builders between 1878 and 1904.

Fig 24. The straight clean lines of Thirlestane Road, constructed between 1878 and 1904.

Photograph by A.C. Robson

The character of the western half of the street is rather different in that the tenement buildings have been constructed on the north side only, overlooking the grounds of St. Margaret's Convent. The scene is now one of elegance and tranquillity and gives not a clue to the complications which arose more than a hundred years ago before even the first stone had been laid. Before 1869 not a single Marchmont tenement had been built. Open fields with clusters of farm buildings were commonplace, and the only buildings of any significance were Bruntsfield House, Greenhill Cottage and St. Margaret's Convent. Whitehouse Loan existed, but only as a narrow sylvan lane, between ancient trees. But the rural setting and seclusion which were so much appreciated by the Convent Community were not to remain for much longer. Their concern was ably described by one of their number:

> The Greenhill Parks (purchased by Dr. Gillis) were feued for buildings, and rows of villas in every style of architecture were

erected opposite the convent. The old trees were cut down and the shady lane which had been such a pleasant approach to the convent, no longer existed. Still, there were the Warrender Parks, and surely they would never be touched! Alas for the uncertainty of human things. The Reverend Mother received intelligence that these beautiful fields were also to be feued for building purposes and that if the Community wished to escape a row of houses close to their boundary wall on the north side their only means of protection was by purchasing a portion of the land in question.

The price was £4,038: 8/-. The feu charter was signed on 21.5.1875, and thus the Community put between it and the prospective purchasers of Thirlestane Road 'part of the lands of Bruntisfield extending to 3 acres and 362 decimal parts of an acre or thereby Imperial Standard measure'. The feu duty was 1p if asked. The Community was delighted. As soon as the purchase of the field was concluded, it was solemnly blessed by the Bishop in a very striking ceremony. The pupils were dressed in white and wore long veils. They carried a banner of the Blessed Virgin, and the Community followed with the banners of St. Joseph and of the Sacred Heart. The Bishop was vested in cape and mitre. The procession went all round the field singing the Hymn of the Sacred Heart, the Litany of the Blessed Virgin and the Hymn of St. Joseph, the Bishop blessing the field with holy water and the usual prayers.

Then the wall was built. But not on the boundary. Indeed no. The feu charter between Sir George Warrender and the Convent Community contained a few conditions which were designed to facilitate the building of Thirlestane Road and to maintain the character of the neighbourhood. The road was to be built half on the land belonging to Sir George and half on the land which the Community had just acquired from Sir George. In return Sir George undertook to pay to the Community the average grass rent for their half until the road was built and, when it was built, to give back to the Community the turf and soil from their half of the road to be laid wherever directed. A further clause, presumably not

E

directed at the Sisters' expected mode of living, declared that the new piece of ground was not to be used as a brewery, distillery, crackling house, slaughter house, public house or to deposit any dungheaps, nuisances or obstructions.

Beside the high Convent wall and about opposite No. 82 Thirlestane Road, there is to this day an interesting clue to yet another problem which beset Sir George and the builders. Firmly embedded in the pavement and only a few inches from the wall are two flat square stones with the numbers 7 and 9 cut into their face. When Sir George Warrender decided to feu out the Warrender Parks, he would be well aware that the City of Edinburgh received its water supply from the natural springs at Swanston and Comiston, and that the old supply pipes running to Castlehill crossed his land. It was discovered that the five-inch pipe from Comiston and the seven-inch pipe from Swanston ran obliquely across the line of a number of proposed streets, and that the pipes were laid too near the surface to be properly arched. In January 1878 an agreement was reached between Sir George and the Edinburgh and District Water Trustees to have the pipes diverted so as to follow the line of Thirlestane Road, Spottiswoode Street and into Warrender Park Terrace. The work was done at the expense of Sir George Warrender, but as it was also proposed to increase the size of the new pipes to seven inches and nine inches, the Water Trustees agreed to pay the difference in costs. The numbers 7 and 9 still seen in Thirlestane Road denote the line of these pipes, and the old markings 5 and 7 can be seen in Strathearn Road near St. Margaret's Tower.

Warrender Baths and Warrender Baths Club

For many people, particularly the younger generation, Thirlestane Road is of course the home of Warrender Baths. In 1886 Frank Y. Henderson formed the Warrender Private Baths Company Ltd., which feued a piece of ground fronting Thirlestane Road from Sir George Warrender for the purpose

Fig 25.   Warrender Baths, ever popular as it nears its centenary.

Photograph by Trevor E.R. Yerbury

of erecting private baths. The Company's registered capital was £8,000 and the baths were erected and equipped at a cost of £11,000, the architect being Robert Paterson, a local resident in Strathearn Road.

On the afternoon of Saturday 17th December, 1887 the baths were formally opened by Sir George Warrender of Lochend, the official ceremony being followed by a display by members of Dennistoun Baths Club, Glasgow.

The baths were superbly equipped with retiring and reading rooms, a billiards room, turkish and plunge baths, a gymnasium and a pond complete with travelling rings and trapeze, all ably supervised by Mr. Watt the first baths master. Membership was £2 2/- and Life Membership was available for the sum of £15 15/-. Elaborate rules and bye-laws controlled the members, and no effort was spared to ensure that the baths would be a sports club of the highest standard.

The founders of Warrender Baths Club in 1888 were mainly members of the Whitehouse Tennis Club, whose courts were situated immediately behind the baths. The first really good swimmer to join the club was an Englishman from Northampton named Joe Baillie. His stroke technique was copied by the top swimmers of the day, among whom was S.J. Aarons, an Australian who was captain of the Water Polo team. S.J. Aarons presented the club with its first trophy — the Aarons Medal — which is still the subject of annual competition by club members. By 1896, the club was at the forefront of Scottish water polo, five members of the team playing in the Scottish trials that year. The following year saw the inception of the Scottish Water Polo Championship, Warrender beating Bon Accord, Aberdeen in the final and becoming the first ever Scottish champions.

In 1906 the retirement of prominent swimmers resulted in a considerable reduction in both enthusiasm and club members, as a result of which the private baths Company was forced to close. During its lifetime the company paid one dividend only of 3% to its shareholders, and at the end of the day the shares were without value.

In 1908 Edinburgh Corporation purchased the baths and all the equipment for £3,000, thereby giving Warrender Baths Club a new lease of life. James H. McCracken, who was assistant pondmaster at the reopening, then began a long and illustrious career as trainer and coach to the club, at all times stressing the importance of adequate coaching for youngsters. His foresight has been a legacy enjoyed by the club ever since. In 1908 Warrender swimmers achieved their first success in the East of Scotland Team Championships, a position which they have virtually monopolised ever since.

Miss Ellen King, a pupil of James Gillespie's High School, became in the 1920s one of the greatest British swimmers of all time and represented Britain at two Olympic Games. She was followed by Miss Jean McDowall, who also represented Britain at the Olympic Games. These high standards have also been maintained in more recent years. In 1970, at the Commonwealth Games in Edinburgh, ten Warrender swimmers were in the Scottish team, and in 1972 Warrender swimmer David Wilkie won an Olympic Silver Medal in the 200 metres breast stroke at Munich. David Wilkie of course went on in 1976 to achieve the supreme accolade by winning the Olympic Gold Medal in the 200 metres breast stroke in Montreal. At the following Olympics in Moscow in 1980 Alan McClatchey and Gordon Downie won bronze medals. In 1981 a distinguished Warrender member, Mrs. Mae Cochrane, O.B.E., was appointed President of the Scottish Amateur Swimming Association.

In 1980 the club became the first in Scotland to appoint a full-time professional coach but lack of funds prevented the club from renewing the contract. Although this was a major disappointment, the club still hopes to engage part-time professional coaching, provided that sufficient financial assistance can be obtained, thereby keeping Warrender in the forefront of the world of swimming.

Thirlestane Lane

To the south of Thirlestane Road and lying along the southern boundary of the Warrender estate is Thirlestane Lane. Although it gives the appearance of being very much older than the rest of Marchmont, it was, in fact, built at about the same time, but its 'old world' appearance has been maintained to the present day. Now designated a private road, it gives access to a number of very elegant mews properties occupied by an interesting group of people, whose amenity is protected by the Thirlestane Lane Association. It is a most attractive street with a variety of south-facing frontages. Its narrow pavement, cobbled road surface, washing poles and miniature gardens give it an atmosphere quite different from the neighbouring streets; but then it has always had a special character of its own. In its heyday it must have been a kaleidoscope of sights and sounds, reflecting a wide spectrum of society. Constructed between 1878 and 1896, it housed the horses, the coaches and the coachmen for the big houses of the

Grange. Within the stables and the harness rooms, there would be that compelling aroma of leather, of straw, and of horses, and outside there were the dung pits built against the boundary wall.

The coachmen and their families lived above the stables, forming a close community, sharing a common life style and contending with unsocial hours. One of the last coachmen to reside there was Mr. Innes, every inch a coachman, with high buttoned coat and rather austere countenance. In those days, of course, before the popularity of the motor car, the coachmen would need to rise early to prepare the coach and horses for the day's work. Many of the owners were important and influential men working in the City who would require to be collected from their houses in the morning and taken back in the evening at the end of their day's work. But all that has gone: that is to say, almost all. To this day, one stable remains, complete with horses, and until recently a clutch of farm livestock strutted and pecked between the worn cobbles. A solitary link with a bygone age.

Although little is known of the coachmen and the stable-lads, history has recorded much of the fortunes of the people for whom they worked.

The earliest development in the Lane was in 1878 when Thomas Crowe the builder erected a stable and coachman's house at No. 6 at the same time as he constructed part of Thirlestane Road. It was built for John Romanes, a solicitor, of Oswald Road, and to this day it is still in the hands of the Romanes Family Trust. Within the next few years stables and houses were built on each side, No. 5 being the property of the Scott sisters of 6 Blackford Road and Nos. 7 and 8 belonging to Col. Dickson who lived in the old house of Morelands, now part of the Astley Ainslie Hospital in Grange Loan. The present occupier of No. 7 is the daughter of Mr. McDonald, who was head gardener to the Bowhills of Morelands before it came within the administration of the hospital.

In 1884 the Lane began to see the first of the small businesses being set up, No. 9 being taken by James Staig Duncan the cabinetmaker and upholsterer. A few years later he moved to larger premises at Nos. 2, 3 and 4, where the business still exists, though not in the hands of the original family. When Mr. Duncan moved out of No. 9 in 1893, extensive alterations were made to convert it into a stable and coach-house for Harry Armour. He was Manager of the Scottish Accident Insurance Co. Ltd., an early progenitor of the modern General Accident Group, and he used the stable to further his interest in the Linlithgow and Stirlingshire Hunt. At the end of an exhausting day at the Hunt in the countryside around Linlithgow, Harry Armour and his daughters would be faced with the long and arduous journey back to Edinburgh in the days before motorised transport and horse boxes were popular. The established procedure was to put the horses on the train at Linlithgow Station and travel with them to Haymarket, where the beasts were unloaded and taken through the Edinburgh streets back to their stable at Thirlestane. Even then there was much to be done with three horses which had spent the greater part of the day in the open countryside. Cleaning and grooming, woollen leg bandages and a feed of warm bran-mash were all standard practice before turning in for the night. Not only was Harry Armour a very practical horseman, but he also spent much of his time contributing to the columns of *Land and Water* under the *nom de plume* 'Palafox', until his sudden death one afternoon at the end of a more than usually boisterous day at the Hunt. Palafox had become a reality.

Harry Armour lived at Flodden Lodge near the Bore Stone in Morningside Road, and later Ashfield in Chamberlain Road, the site of the private burial ground of John Livingston, owner of Greenhill who died of the plague in 1645. The owner of another interesting property nearby, Clinton House, had a small stable built at No. 1 in 1885, this property being substantially altered over the years to house the Falcon Motor Co., W.T. Dunbar & Son, and now the Marchmont Garage.

In 1887 two feus in the Lane (Nos. 10 and 11) were developed as private dwelling houses only, without any stables built at street level. Probably intended for the use of domestic staff, these houses were owned by Duncan McLaren Jnr., who had just had built for himself, a few years earlier, the large detached property of St. Oswalds in Oswald Road. Duncan McLaren Jnr. was a very successful businessman, son of Duncan McLaren Snr., Member of Parliament and Lord Provost of Edinburgh, of Newington House near Minto Street, whose name is commemorated in the streets nearby, Duncan Street and McLaren Road.

Lord Provosts, or perhaps more accurately, photographs of them, occasionally turn up in the most unexpected places. When the BBC, in London, were arranging to bury a time capsule depicting life on earth in 1982, the BBC in Edinburgh were running an interesting story on a time capsule which had been found in an old building in McLeod Street in Edinburgh. The capsule had been placed in the foundation stone of a small housing development at Dalry Meadows on 4.6.1896 by Mrs. McDonald, wife of the Right Hon. Andrew McDonald, Lord Provost of the City of Edinburgh. In it there was a most interesting collection of papers, coins and plans, which have been preserved by the Gorgie and Dalry Housing Association, but perhaps the most interesting item was a photograph of the Lord and Lady Provost. When Andrew McDonald was Lord Provost of Edinburgh he lived at 40 Lauder Road, and every morning his coachman left Thirlestane Lane punctually to call for the Provost to take him on his tour of duty. By 1947, long after the death of Sir Andrew, the early morning tour of duty had lost many of the trappings of high office, because Sir Andrew's coach-house at No. 11a was then used as 'a district muster room to house overnight six street orderly barrows of modern design'.

During the 1890s the last five feus in the Lane were developed by a number of prominent businessmen of the time. No. 13 was built for George Ritchie of Braidfoot in Grange Loan, a principal in the firm of G. Ritchie & Son, Bells Brewery in the Pleasance, and No. 14 was built for Harry W. Smith, a solicitor, of Norwood; it now forms part of the

Fig 26. Sir Andrew McDonald, Lord Provost of Edinburgh, 1894–97; Master of the Merchant Company, 1888–90.

Courtesy of Gorgie/Dalry Housing Association Ltd.

Fig 27. Mrs. McDonald, wife of Sir Andrew McDonald, Lord Provost of Edinburgh.

Courtesy of Gorgie/Dalry Housing Association Ltd.

Royal Bank of Scotland complex in Kilgraston Road. A few years later in 1896 identical properties, Nos. 15 and 16, were built for two partners in a firm of stockbrokers, R.S.L. Hardie of Grange Terrace and G.B. Turnbull of Mansionhouse Road.

The Lane was completed in 1896 by the construction of No. 17, a stable, coach-house and private dwelling, for Gersham Gourlay of Airlie Lodge, Whitehouse Loan who moved to Edinburgh after retiring from a successful career as an engineer and shipowner in Dundee.

CHAPTER 5

Spottiswoode, Arden and Lauderdale

Marchmont was built in two fairly distinct phases on either side of the year 1900. The original part was built between 1878–1900 to include the streets which lie generally to the east and to the north of Warrender Park Road. The early phase of building was characterised by the individual nature of the architect's plans, drawn in the Scottish Baronial style as required by the terms of the feu charters. But by 1900 this style had given way to long straight facades of identical buildings in most of the streets south of Warrender Park Road. That is not to say that the new buildings were in any way inferior to those built at the end of the nineteenth century. Indeed, although the houses in and around Arden Street have no special architectural interest, they were constructed of very good quality polished ashlar from the quarries of Blaxter and Denwick. What they perhaps lack in exterior detail is more than made up in the high quality finish of these elegant flats. This is the land of the 'wally closes' of Spottiswoode, where mosaics and bevelled tiles replace concrete and cement plaster. It was to Spottiswoode that Professor David Daiches was taken as a small boy on endless visits to friends and relations at a time when he thought there were many more interesting things to do. In his book *Two Worlds* he captures the mood in his inimitable style with the words, 'it seemed to me that there were people who like the Mad Hatter, the March Hare and the Dormouse were perpetually having tea and that other people wandered in and out among the cups and saucers at will'.

Building on the South Park

The streets of Spottiswoode, Arden and Lauderdale were built on what was originally the South Park of the Lands of

Fig 28. The camera lens brings Edinburgh Castle to the foot of Spottiswoode Street.

Photograph by Hugh Fraser

Bruntisfield, but with the exception of the north end of Spottiswoode Street they did not feature at all in the Bryce Feuing Plan of 1869. However, in 1876 when Watherston came to realign the intended position of some of the streets, the decision had already been taken to feu all the land in the North Park and the South Park. If the Watherston plans had been fully implemented, then Spottiswoode Road would have been extended, to the west, through the Bruntsfield House policy grounds to meet Whitehouse Loan near where Bruntsfield Hospital now stands. The plans were implemented with only minor variations, although some street names were subject to alteration. Arden Street was originally named Alvanley Street (the change being made when Marchmont Terrace was renamed Alvanley Terrace), and Lauderdale Street would have been named Spottiswoode Terrace if the Town Clerk's suggestion had been accepted in 1908.

When the first phase of Marchmont was being built, there

were a number of disputes between the speculative builders and the owners of existing property who felt that their amenity was threatened by the new development. However, this was not a problem during the second phase because, by and large, the South Park had been open farmland under lease from Sir George Warrender and there were very few buildings of a permanent nature on the land. In fact as late as 1900 only the north side of Warrender Park Road had been built, and the occupiers of the flats had an uninterrupted view over the corn fields of the South Park right up to Thirlestane Road. On the south side of Warrender Park Road an old stone wall ran along the line of the existing pavement with one or two gateways giving access to the fields. The Iron Church for Warrender Park Free Church was flourishing, the Usher Institute feu was just being pegged out, and the surveyors were beginning to take measurements for the alignment of Arden Street, Spottiswoode Street, Spottiswoode Road, and Lauderdale Street.

But there were no plans to build in the same way and in the same style as the first phase. No individual designs were submitted. No small building associations were formed and no single feus were developed. It was the era of the big builder who constructed whole streets at a time, and frequently to the same design. In fact most of the second phase was completed between 1902 and 1916 by no more than four separate builders.

Arden Street was constructed between 1905 and 1911 by two members of the Cruikshank family who were well-known builders in Edinburgh around that time. George Cruikshank started building at the south end in 1905, and William S. Cruikshank started building at the north end in the same year. Whilst there is no doubt that the masons married the two facades in perfect harmony, it is said that the missing numbers on each side of the street are evidence that the two members of the Cruikshank family did not see eye-to-eye and had not taken the precaution to ensure that the numbers did not follow a similar fate.

Fig 29. Arden Street — the Cruikshank family 'married' the facades in perfect harmony.
Photograph by A.C. Robson

Although the corner sections of Spottiswoode Road were constructed by John Souden in 1887 and 1899 (when he was completing Marchmont Road), the remainder of Spottiswoode Road was not finished until about 1914. The work was done by George Cruikshank, John Souden and Kinnear Moodie & Co., but the idea to link Spottiswoode Road with Whitehouse Loan was never implemented. Spottiswoode Street (south of Warrender Park Road) was built in a similar fashion between 1902 and 1911, the whole of the west side by John Souden and the whole of the east side by William S. Cruikshank. On the short section leading onto Thirlestane Road, near No. 97 Spottiswoode Street, are the initials RC, the date 1900 and the Scottish thistle carved into the stonework, commemorating Robert Chisholm, the builder, who was involved with his partner John Davidson in the construction of Thirlestane Road.

Whilst it may be difficult to say exactly which tenement was the last to be completed, the indications are that it was in

Lauderdale Street, probably around No. 33. Certainly these
were the last plans to be approved by the Dean of Guild Court
on 9.2.1911, and the feu charter was not signed until 5.8.1915,
suggesting that occupation of the building would be sometime
in the early part of 1916. As with Arden Street, George
Cruikshank started at the top end in 1910, and William S.
Cruikshank started at the bottom end in 1911. It is not known
if they had patched up their differences, but they certainly
matched up their numbers, all of which are in sequence except
No. 13, which, presumably in deference to superstition, has
been numbered 11A.

The South Park Quarries

Although Sir George Warrender's estate lay on well-drained,
arable land, part of it, and part of the surrounding estates, had
been used in the past to quarry stones for the construction of
the older parts of Edinburgh. By the time the land had been
feued for building purposes, the quarries were more or less
extinct, but they still posed a considerable problem because
they had not been filled in and, in any case, would require a
lengthy period of consolidation before being suitable for the
construction of a four-storey Scottish tenement. There was a
group of such quarries on that part of Bruntsfield Links just
opposite Alvanley Terrace, but they did not pose any great
threat as no building was to be constructed on the Links. In
fact they were partially filled in around the time that W. & D.
McGregor was building Warrender Park Crescent, although
traces of them can still be seen today.

There is no evidence to suggest that stone from these old
quarries was actually used in the construction of the front
elevations of the Marchmont tenements. Indeed, the feu
charters frequently named the quarries from which the stone
was to be obtained, and many of these were in
Northumberland. The same charters did, however, recognise
that there was local stone available and permitted a certain

depth of quarrying to be done as the construction of the tenements progressed. It can be assumed therefore that a fair amount of local stone was used where appearance and durability were not so important.

But the quarries which created the greatest problem were those which lay in the line of a proposed street or where foundations were to be laid. The Dean of Guild records indicate quite clearly that when Warrender Park Terrace was being constructed one hundred years ago, the Burgh Engineer was required to point out to prospective developers and architects that the site was that of a disused quarry and that special provisions would require to be made for extra strength in the foundations. In the construction of Arden Street in 1906 William S. Cruikshank also had to make special arrangements for the laying of drains in view of the difficulties encountered with a bed of solid rock not far from the surface.

Until the last few years of the nineteenth century the only tenement on the south side of Warrender Park Road was the block on the corner with Marchmont Road which had been built in 1888 by Hugh Mackintosh. Just to the west of that tenement and at a point near what is now No. 70 Warrender Park Road there was a wooden gate set into the old stone wall, giving access to the field behind Marchmont Road. It was here that the builders had the greatest problems because a huge quarry sat completely astride the line of the proposed tenements on the west side of Marchmont Road. Although the quarry had not been in use for a number of years, some old buildings still remained, and consolidation of the infill would take many years. The unaffected part of Marchmont Road had been completed in 1890, but the remainder of the site lay empty for ten years before John Souden attempted to build on it. Even then special arrangements were necessary, with Sir George Warrender agreeing to pay £100 compensation to the builder for the extra cost of each foundation, 'which sum shall not be payable until the foundations of the houses have been properly laid out and built clear of the surface of the ground to the satisfaction of James Watherston, Builder'. As the quarry was large enough to impinge on the frontage of Spottiswoode Road, a further payment of £50 compensation was allowed for special foundations if they were found to be necessary. As the tenements progressed, the old stone wall round the quarry was demolished and the stone was used as bottoming in the construction of Spottiswoode Road.

The Warrender Mystery

Spottiswoode might well be considered one of the youngest parts of Marchmont; nevertheless it still holds the secret of a mystery which has remained unsolved for almost four hundred years. To get some idea of the origin of the story it is necessary to go back in time: back much further than the span of human memory. Although accurate accounts of 'Marchmont' at the beginning of the seventeenth century are not readily obtainable, we are fortunate that the mood of the moment was captured by Margaret Warrender and recorded in her book entitled *Walks near Edinburgh*. She was writing in 1895 when the impact of the new Marchmont was at its greatest, and she was quietly reflecting on what had been, in former times. Her words are worth recalling:

> Let us call back the past as it was two hundred and fifty years ago, and what a different scene rises before our eyes; an open undulating muirland, covered with whin and broom and with thickets of thorn and natural oak growing in the more sheltered hollows. This is the great Boroughmuir which stretches far away to the hills of Braid and in more remote times formed part of the ancient forest of Drumselch. A long winding loch lies between us and the town, in the low ground which future generations were to call the Meadows. . . .

A tranquil scene, but not one which gives any indication of the curse of the day — the terrible plague which swept through Edinburgh on more than one occasion in the seventeenth century. In those days there was no Usher Institute to control public health, but instead there were the Statuts for the Baillies of the Mure which enacted, among other things, that victims of the plague were forbidden the rites of sepulture with their kindred. Instead they were buried on the Burgh Muir. Hear the words of the statute in 1568:

> That with all deligence possible, sa sone as ony houss sall be infectit, the haill houshald, with their gudds, be depescit, towert the mure, the deid buriet, and with like deligence the houss clengit.

That people were buried on the Mure is beyond doubt, but who they were and when they died is lost in the mists of time; lost ... or at any rate obscured by progress. But their plight has never been ignored by writers in Edinburgh. In fact the Warrender Tombstone has probably been mentioned by every eminent writer on the south side of Edinburgh: Grant, Wilson, Mair, Smith and many more. Wilson says, 'Here amid the pasturage of the Meadow and within sight of the busy capital a large flat tombstone may be seen, time worn and grey with the moss of age; it bears on it a skull surmounted by a winged sandglass and a scroll inscribed MORS PACE HORA CAELI, and below this is a shield bearing a saltire with the initials M.I.R. and the date of the fatal year 1645. The M surmounts the shield and in all probability indicates that the deceased had taken his degree of Master of Arts'. Grant also refers to the tombstone, but for some reason which is not explained he reproduces in Volume III, under the caption 'Old Tombstone at Warrender Park', the drawing of a stone with the date 1645, the initials I.L. and the inscription 'Mors patet hora latet' (Death is most sure, unseen its hour). From the other information given in Grant it is almost certain that he has confused this stone with that which still lies in Chamberlain Road marking the grave of John Livingston, and which is dealt with in some detail by Charles J. Smith in his book *Historic South Edinburgh*. Certainly Mair suggests that the Warrender stone (with the initials I.R.) commemorates a member of the Rig family who owned Rigsland before it was

F

Fig 30.   Grant maintained that this was the Warrender Tombstone of 1645, with the initials I.L. 'Victorian romance'?

From Grant's Old & New Edinburgh. *See Fig 31*

Fig 31.   The genuine stone photographed in the grounds of Bruntsfield House *circa* 1950. The boring truth!

Courtesy of Miss A.B. Laidlaw. Photograph by C. McKenzie. See Fig 30

incorporated in the Warrender estates. It is known that Rigsland was owned in 1645 by John Rig, an advocate in Edinburgh.

The stone lay in the South Park for more than two hundred years before Marchmont was built, but in the late nineteenth century it was moved to make way for the new tenements. Thanks to the foresight of the Warrender family, it was carefully removed from the place of interment and placed against an old wall which marked the east boundary of the Bruntsfield House garden. At that time Margaret Warrender confirms that some of the carvings could still be traced, and as recently as the 1950s the stone was photographed in the recessed wall near Lauderdale Street. By the early 1960s it was found that the stone lay in the path of the new James Gillespie's High School, but by then it was more than three hundred years old and was in no condition for another journey. The ravages of time had obliterated all reference to a secular life, and it disintegrated on being moved. The pieces lie buried beneath the School.

Such then is the story of the Warrender Tombstone; its mystery solved; solved that is, provided we ignore the evidence from the old maps of Edinburgh which have always insisted that the Warrender stone had a date 1596.

CHAPTER 6

Alvanley and Whitehouse

In the days before the Warrender estates and the Greenhill estates had been feued by their owners, the roadway which we now know as Alvanley Terrace and Whitehouse Loan was not much more than a rough track giving access to Viewpark, Bruntsfield House, Greenhill Cottage and the Whitehouse. The old tree-lined loaning was, however, dramatically altered in character when the houses of Greenhill and Marchmont were built. The section of Alvanley Terrace (previously Marchmont Terrace) on which there are now a number of hotels was chosen by Sir George Warrender and David Bryce, the architect, as the starting point of the original plan of 1869. As it turned out, the few terraced houses Nos. 2, 3 and 4 are all that was ever constructed of the Bryce plans. Today, although the roadway is now a busy through-road to the Grange and Church Hill, it has retained a number of interesting features in harmony with the more modern development around it.

Scottish Youth Hostels Association

Inveni portum — 'I have found a haven'. Such is the motto and policy of the Scottish Youth Hostels Association, founded in Edinburgh in 1931 by a group of enthusiasts led by Dr. Alan Fothergill. At a meeting on 13.2.1931 under the chairmanship of Lord Salvesen the Association was inaugurated 'to help all but especially young people of limited means living and working in industrial and other areas, to know, use and appreciate the Scottish countryside and places of historic and cultural interest in Scotland, and to promote their health, recreation and education, particularly by providing simple hostel accommodation for them on their travels'. That there

Fig 32. The terraced houses of the Bryce Feuing Plan 1869, in Alvanley Terrace.

Photograph by A.C. Robson

are still such 'havens' throughout Scotland available for all who enjoy the outdoor life is a credit to the men and women who, over the years, have put so much effort into maintaining the original ideals of the Association.

The driving force behind the inauguration of the Association was undoubtedly Dr. Fothergill who, despite his ill-health, worked ceaselessly to establish the Association in its early days. However, in 1934 he resigned from his position as Honorary Secretary when his National Executive accepted an offer of reciprocity from the German Youth Hostels Association which, in the eyes of Fothergill, was controlled for political propaganda by the Nazi Government of Germany. That break was to prove a tragic loss to the Association, because in the following year Dr. Fothergill died at the very early age of 37.

Despite this early loss, District Committees were soon set up in Glasgow, Edinburgh, Dundee and Aberdeen and, in May 1931, the first youth hostel was opened at Broadmeadows near Selkirk. In the first five years tremendous advances were made

Fig 33. Dignitaries at the opening of Broadmeadows Youth Hostel, 1931.
Courtesy of Scottish Youth Hostels Association

in setting up new hostels and in building up new membership all over Scotland.

Although there was a hostel in another part of Edinburgh in the early days of the Association, it was not until 1949 that the Bruntsfield site was secured. After considering a number of other sites, the National Executive decided to purchase the property in Bruntsfield Crescent which until then had been occupied as an hotel. At the time of the semi-jubilee in 1956 the Association organised a celebration walk over the Border hills to Scotland's first hostel at Broadmeadows. Two busloads of members set out from the Bruntsfield Hostel for Traquair to begin the six-mile walk across the Minch Moor to Broadmeadows, no doubt arriving with an appetite capable of doing justice to the special 25th birthday cake which had been prepared for the occasion.

In recent years the hostel at Bruntsfield Crescent has been extensively modernised, and a District Office has been established in Warrender Park Road at the corner with Alvanley Terrace.

Bruntsfield House

To many citizens of Edinburgh, Bruntsfield House is
considered the home of the Warrender family whose name is
commemorated in the street names nearby, namely Warrender
Park Road, Terrace and Crescent. The Warrenders' occupation
of Bruntsfield House certainly represents a significant part of its
history and was of crucial importance in the late nineteenth
century when plans were being considered for the layout of
the new district of Warrender Park. But when an earlier Sir
George Warrender acquired the ownership of Bruntsfield
House in 1695, this 'semi-fortified mansion' had already made
a considerable contribution to the pages of history.

The earliest record of the estate of Bruntsfield is a charter
granted by Robert II in favour of Alan de Lawdre on 4th June
1381, in which it states that, prior to that transaction, the lands
were in the possession of Richard Broune, King's Sergeant of
the Burgh Muir. As King's Sergeant in these early days he
would be expected to assist in the collection of Crown
revenues and to 'summon the lieges' to the King's tribunals,
but it is very doubtful if he ever thought that his name would
still be known in the district more than six hundred years later.
Though greatly altered by usage and the passage of time, it is
now clearly established that the name Broune gave rise firstly
to Brounisfield, then by way of various spellings to
Bruntisfield and finally to Bruntsfield. There was a fanciful
tradition prevalent for many years that the designation was
taken from one Stephen Bruntfield, allegedly murdered on the
Links while being taken a prisoner to the Castle, but as this
suggestion has now been dismissed by the historians as wholly
inaccurate, it is to be hoped that, like the unfortunate victim in
the story, it will now be laid to rest. What is much more
interesting is that the present head of the Warrender family has
adopted the older spelling in his title Lord Bruntisfield of
Boroughmuir. The Lauders maintained ownership of
Bruntsfield House until 1603, except for a short time in the
fifteenth century when the house was in the possession of

Fig 34. Aerial view of Bruntsfield House and James Gillespie's High School.

Courtesy of Scotsman Publications Ltd.

Fig 35. Bruntsfield House, restored in 1966 by Rowand Anderson, Kininmonth & Paul, architects.

Courtesy of A.L. Hunter

Henry Cant, whose family had also been owners of Grange House. In 1603 the house was bought from Sir Alexander Lauder by John Fairlie of Braid, who made a number of additions and improvements to it, the date 1605 and the initials of himself and his wife Elizabethe Westoun being inscribed above the window lintels.

In the closing years of the seventeenth century the Fairlies' occupation of Bruntsfield House was coming to an end, and in 1695 they sold the property and its estates to Sir George Warrender, a successful merchant in the City of Edinburgh. Sir George was Lord Provost of the City in 1713–1714, and in the following year, the year of the '15 Rebellion, he accepted a baronetcy from the newly crowned Hanoverian King George I, thus publicly renouncing any private thoughts which he may have had about supporting the Jacobite cause. The historian Grant, in his work *Old & New Edinburgh,* asserts that the old mansion 'called Bruntsfield or Warrender House was the ancestral seat of a family which got it as a free gift from the magistrates', but this statement is not accurate. The property was never really known as Warrender House, and at no time in its early history was it ever under the control of the City Magistrates. Although completely surrounded by the Burgh Muir, the superiority of which was held by the City, the Bruntsfield Estate was held by the Lauders, the Fairlies and the Warrenders under Crown Charters of Confirmation and Crown Writs of Clare Constat.

It was a later Sir George Warrender, Member of Parliament, who realised the geographical importance of his land in relation to the growth of the City to the south during the latter part of the nineteenth century. He must have been well aware that many parts of the Grange and Greenhill had been feued for building purposes and that the rewards to the superiors were considerable. It was he who engaged David Bryce the architect to draw up the feuing plan of 1869 which was later abandoned in favour of Watherston's more elaborate scheme in 1876. Although Bryce did not live to see the district of Marchmont built, it is evident that towards the end of his life he had already come to the conclusion that his original idea of detached villas and self-contained houses with mews stables should give way to the development of tenement buildings in the Scottish Baronial style. When Sir George died in 1901, much of the building programme had been completed, but when the estate passed to his trustees there was considerable hesitation about the future of Bruntsfield House. For long periods the house remained unoccupied, and concern grew at the possibility of the property being demolished and the ground used for building purposes. When notices to that effect were produced in the district in the early 1930s the matter was referred to a Committee of the Lord Provost to take action to ensure preservation. Fortunately Sir Victor Warrender was sympathetic to the idea of conservation and offered to relinquish his life rent interest in the property in favour of Edinburgh Corporation. The disposition was completed in June 1935 in which it was stated that the ground could only be used for a 'school, hospital, home, museum, art gallery, institute, public hall, public library, public park, recreation ground, swimming baths, public offices, garden, allotments or for any other public or municipal purpose in connection with the welfare of the City of Edinburgh'. The structure of the mansionhouse was to be preserved as a building of historic interest, and although certain additional house building was to be permitted on the south side of Spottiswoode Road and the west side of Lauderdale Street (after a waiting period of twenty years), no building was to be permitted on Whitehouse Loan or Warrender Park Road, in perpetuity. Owing to the Second World War and the shortage of funds thereafter, no decision was made about the site for several years, but in 1963 permission was granted by Edinburgh Corporation for Bruntsfield House to become the centrepiece of the new James Gillespie's School. Thanks to the skill of the architects Rowand Anderson, Kininmonth & Paul, most of the original features of the house have been retained, although a Victorian extension on the east wing was demolished. Unfortunately many of the features of the garden ground have now been lost for ever. The ice-house in the south-east corner of the garden has been filled-in and built over, and the Warrender Tombstone referred to in Chapter 5 disintegrated on being moved. In addition, the Lodge House facing Whitehouse Loan was demolished some years ago, having been the home of Mr. and Mrs. Buchan and their family during the time that Mr. Buchan was gardener to the estate. Progress has therefore taken its toll, but what has been lost is a small price to pay for what has been saved. Bruntsfield House, with roots going back to the fourteenth century, is now restored and taking a central place in the administration of education in Edinburgh.

James Gillespie's High School

There has been a school, in Edinburgh, under the name James Gillespie, since 1803, although during its long and distinguished history it has changed its structure and organisation on many

Fig 36. Gillespie's Hospital, constructed in 1802 and described as 'a tasteless edifice in Carpenters' Gothic'.

occasions. Its origin, however, has never been lost sight of, and each succeeding generation has kept the name in the forefront of Scottish education.

James Gillespie was born in 1726 into comparatively humble surroundings, but through diligence and strict adherence to the now less popular maxim 'waste not want not' he succeeded in building up a very successful business in the snuff trade. Assisted by his elder brother John who ran the retail shop in the High Street, James was not long in gathering around himself the trappings of wealth. He acquired Spylaw House at Colinton along with a snuff mill and settled down to an industrious life as the 'Laird of Colinton'. When he died in 1797, he left the greater part of his fortune for the erection and endowment of a Hospital for aged men and women and a Free School for poor boys, to be managed by the Edinburgh Merchant Company as Trustees.

The Trustees acquired the old mansion of Wrychtishousis in Gillespie Crescent and, much to the consternation of the conservationists of the day, had it demolished to make way for the new Gillespie's Hospital which was opened in 1802. In the

Fig 37. Bust of James Gillespie in the Merchants' Hall, Edinburgh.
Photograph by A.C. Robson

following year the first Gillespie's School was built for boys only, on a site now occupied by tenement buildings in Bruntsfield Place. By 1870 the Hospital system had been discontinued and the boys were transferred to the Gillespie Crescent building, where the school continued on a fee-paying basis for girls and boys. Despite the introduction of the fees, however, the Trustees were unable to cope with the financial problems of upgrading the school, and in 1908 they passed the administration over to the Edinburgh School Board. A few years later in 1914 the Board, having built a new school for Boroughmuir in Viewforth, was then in a position to move

Gillespie's School into the vacated building in Warrender Park Crescent. Still co-educational in 1923, it was found necessary to relieve overcrowding by moving the Junior School out to Warrender Park School in Marchmont Crescent, but this proved to be a temporary expedient only. In 1929 intake at Warrender Park Crescent was limited to girls only, thus establishing James Gillespie's High School for Girls, which for many years stamped the hallmark of education onto an army of girls instantly recognisable by their maroon and gold 'pork pie' hats. The Infant Department moved into a new Annexe in 1936 built on the site of Viewpark Cottage and Studio of Swan Watson. The Primary Department was later transferred to the grounds of Bruntsfield House with the preparatory section established in the house itself, and on the closing of James Gillespie's Boys' School in Marchmont Crescent in 1973 it became co-educational.

Although the proposed new school in the grounds of Bruntsfield House had been considered in the 1930s, shortage of cash and the intervention of the Second World War delayed the project for more than twenty years. However, by the early 1960s a lot of work had gone into planning a new modern school using Bruntsfield House as the centre of the modern complex. The new school was designed by Rowand Anderson, Kininmonth & Paul and opened for pupils in August 1966. By 1973 the school was reorganised again on a non-selective local-intake basis for boys and girls within the concept of the new comprehensive-type school. At the present day the school, under the very able leadership of Dr. Patricia Thomas, is still very conscious of its historical past. Founder's Day is still celebrated, the motto *Fidelis et Fortis* is still to the fore, and the school maintains a significant presence in Scottish education today.

Bruntsfield Hospital

Soon the centenary will be celebrated of a hospital whose very

2 Medical Ward, Bruntsfield Hospital, Edinburgh.

Fig 38. Bruntsfield Hospital Medical Ward, *circa* 1933.
By *courtesy of Miss E.M. Baxter*

existence is steeped in the history of medicine. No doubt the history of Bruntsfield Hospital will be told in greater detail in 1985, but in the meantime a short account of the salient facts may suffice.

Like so many other civic and social achievements of the Victorian era, Bruntsfield Hospital was the brainchild of one person, who knew exactly what she intended to achieve and spent the best part of her life in that endeavour. That she was successful in these endeavours is beyond doubt; that her ideals are still shared by all, is a matter of conjecture.

Miss Sophia Jex-Blake was born in Hastings in 1840. Her first ambition was to become a teacher, but whilst staying with friends attached to a hospital in New England, she decided instead to devote her life to medicine. On arriving in Scotland she would have been well aware that for a young lady to become a teacher in Edinburgh was possible, and was even socially acceptable, but to become a doctor of medicine was quite another matter. In fact it was impossible and would probably have remained so for much longer than it did, had it not been for the determination of Miss Jex-Blake and her contemporaries. That determination never waned during her circuitous route to fame. Although she did attend certain medical classes at Edinburgh University, it was necessary for her to go to Berne to qualify as a Doctor of Medicine, after which she obtained the Licentiateship of the King's and Queen's Colleges in Ireland which enabled her to practise in Great Britain. When she returned to Edinburgh again in 1878, she set up a practice at No. 4 Manor Place and a dispensary for women in Grove Street, which by 1885 was elevated to the status of a small 'hospital' by the provision of a few beds. In 1898 the patients were transferred to Bruntsfield Lodge, the home of Dr. Jex-Blake, which became the first Bruntsfield Hospital for Women and Children. Shortly thereafter she retired to the south of England where she died in 1912.

Her pioneering spirit, however, lived on long after her retirement. On 18th July 1911 Queen Mary opened the new Bruntsfield Hospital with the additional accommodation of the Beilby Ward and the Venters Ward. Not only was it a great day of celebration for the medical staff at Bruntsfield, but also for the many people from Marchmont who turned out to see the Queen and her entourage driving down Warrender Park Road, at the conclusion of the ceremony. As the Queen passed the bottom of Lauderdale Street she would, no doubt, be conscious of the impromptu civic reception area, constructed at very short notice, by the joiners and other tradesmen who were still working on the tenement buildings. While the roughly built timber platform may not have had the usual trappings of purple and gold, it certainly provided a grandstand view of the Royal procession.

At the present day, within the ambit of the National Health Service, Bruntsfield continues to serve the community as a hospital specially adapted to the needs of women and children.

Warrender Church

Almost a century ago, when the Rev. Thomas Currie was still

building up his congregation at the small Iron Church in Warrender Park Road, he was ever mindful that the day would soon come when a more permanent building would be required as his church grew in strength and influence. The original Iron Church designed by D.A. Robertson in 1885 was capable of seating about four hundred people, but within a comparatively short time overcrowding had become a problem. Fortunately, a very eminent architect, Thomas P. Marwick, had moved into a house at No. 1 Spottiswoode Street and volunteered to draw up plans for two small transepts to increase the capacity of the church by about two hundred. But there still remained a lack of permanence, because the site on which the church stood had been secured on a short lease only, from Sir George Warrender. It soon became obvious to the Kirk Session that a site would require to be found for the erection of a new stone church. After refusing first option on the site later developed as the Usher Institute in Warrender Park Road, and after considering at least two other possibilities, a decision was taken to secure the vacant ground at the corner of Whitehouse Loan and Greenhill Terrace. Plans were drawn up by the architect R. Macfarlane Cameron for a handsome edifice in the Italian Renaissance style, and the foundation stone was laid on 23.5.1891 by Professor A.R. Simpson, M.D. The silver trowel used in the ceremony was gifted by Mr. Cameron, the architect. The church was opened for public worship on a Thursday, 2.6.1892, by Rev. Dr. J. Monro Gibson of London, and the first Sunday service was taken by Professor Blaikie, described by J.W.E. Gladstone as the true father of Warrender. Prof. Blaikie had, of course, been a member of the interim Kirk Session for the Iron Church in 1884 at a time when he was already committed to a number of other public duties.

In making the transfer to the stone church, Rev. Thomas Currie was not, of course, starting a new congregation, and it was therefore possible for all the existing organisations in the church to continue without any significant interruption. The Kirk Session had always made a special point of being

G

Fig 39. Warrender Park Church, built in 1891 to replace the Iron Church in Warrender Park Road.
Courtesy of Miss Wilma Gladstone

receptive to the needs of young people, and particularly the many students who lived in digs in Marchmont even as long ago as 1890. The students were given special seat concessions in the new church and were encouraged to attend the many open-air services which were held on Bruntsfield Links.

When Rev. John Hall was appointed minister in 1899, his first major event was, of course, the Union of the Free Church of Scotland and the United Presbyterian Church in October 1900, following which the congregation took the name of Warrender Park United Free Church. The name was greatly simplified to Warrender Church in 1929 at the time of the Union of the United Free Church with the Established Church. It may have remained under that name to this day but for the decision of the congregation to enter into a Union in 1972 with West St. Giles Church and Grange Church to form the new congregation of Marchmont St. Giles. On completion of the Union the new congregation used the former Grange Church for worship and, at the time of writing, the elegant

Fig 40. St. Margaret's Convent with the Chapel designed by Gillespie Graham.

Photograph by A.C. Robson

Italian Renaissance building of the former Warrender Church faces an uncertain future.

St. Margaret's Convent

When Pope John Paul visited Edinburgh in May 1982, it was generally considered that, with a few exceptions, he was welcomed with warm affection by the citizens of Edinburgh, both Catholic and Protestant. A far cry from the days of the Reformation, the mood of which seemed to be far from the minds of the people of Marchmont and Grange who stood three or four deep, one summer evening, in Strathearn Road to see the Holy Father drive past at a speed much greater than the majority of their cameras. Fortunately, on the following evening Pope John Paul's itinerary was sufficiently relaxed to allow an extravaganza of informality at the gates of St. Bennet's, the house of Cardinal Gray in Strathearn Place. But such apparent tolerance has not always been a feature of religion in Scotland.

In 1834 Edinburgh was in no mood to welcome the Head of the Roman Catholic Church, even if such a foolhardy suggestion had been made. Even those who were considered forward in their thinking came to the conclusion that the founding of a new convent in Scotland was, to say the least, premature. However, that was not a view which was shared by the Rev. James Gillis, a devout Roman Catholic curate, born of Scottish parents in Montreal, who returned to Scotland with a determination to fulfil his vision of a Catholic community in his native land. His zeal and determination were recognised and taken up by two young intrants to the Order of the Ursulines of Jesus at Chevagnes in France. They too had strong Scottish connections. One intrant, the daughter of a minister of the Church of Scotland, was Miss Agnes Trail who was converted to the Catholic faith whilst visiting Rome in 1828 in her study of art and painting. Her conversion to Catholicism at that time attracted a great deal of attention because hitherto she had been spoken of as 'the lady that went to Rome to convert the Pope'. The other intrant was Miss Margaret Clapperton, the daughter of an old Catholic family from Fochabers in Morayshire. However, to build a convent in Scotland in 1834 required more than zeal and determination. It required money. Fortunately the enthusiasm of Rev. Gillis and his followers was more than matched by the generosity of John Menzies of Pitfodels in Aberdeenshire, whose timely gift made possible the purchase of an old manor house and grounds known for many years previously as the Whitehouse, in what is now Whitehouse Loan. In those days the surrounding estates were in the possession of Mrs. Ann Grant, widow of Francis Grant of Kilgraston in Perthshire, and the old house had already earned itself a not inconsiderable place in the history of the Burgh Muir (described in fascinating detail by Charles J. Smith in his work *Historic South Edinburgh*). In 1834 Whitehouse was purchased for the sum of £3,000, and work began on planning the foundation of the first convent to be

Fig 41. Pope John Paul and the Sisters of St. Margaret's Convent.
Courtesy of St. Margaret's Convent

built in Scotland since the Reformation. Whilst there can be no doubt about the piety and devotion of James Gillis and his team from Chevagnes, their early days at the Whitehouse raised a number of essentially practical problems. In fact, so unsuitable was the old manor house for immediate living accommodation that the Sisters took up the offer of alternative accommodation for a few months in the house of Mr. and Mrs. Stevenson. The house was Argyle Park, a substantial property which stood in Argyle Place before the tenement buildings were erected. In these formative days another constant source of encouragement was Sir George Warrender of Bruntsfield House who, although not of the Catholic faith, was happy to accept the Community as his neighbours and to allow them access to his estate around Bruntsfield House. Despite the early difficulties, substantial progress was made in establishing all the essentials of conventual life, with the magnificent chapel being erected in 1835 to a design by the celebrated architect of the time, Gillespie Graham.

Fig 42. Pope John Paul and the Scottish Hierarchy at St. Bennet's, May 1982. Reading from left to right: Right Rev. Joseph Devine, Bishop of Motherwell; Right Rev. Joseph McGee, former Bishop of Galloway, R.I.P.; Right Rev. William Hart, former Bishop of Dunkeld (retired); Right Rev. Stephen McGill, Bishop of Paisley; Right Rev. Vincent Logan, Bishop of Dunkeld; Right Rev. Charles Renfrew, Bishop and Auxiliary Glasgow (nearest to the Pope); Right Rev. Francis Thomson, former Bishop of Motherwell (retired); Pope John Paul; His Eminence Cardinal Gordon Gray, Archbishop of St. Andrews and Edinburgh; Most Reverend Thomas Winning, Archbishop of Glasgow; Right Rev. Mario Conti, Bishop of Aberdeen; Right Rev. Colin MacPherson, Bishop of Argyll and the Isles; Right Rev. Maurice Taylor, Bishop of Galloway; Right Rev. James Monaghan, Auxiliary Bishop of Edinburgh.

Photograph by courtesy of St. Margaret's Convent

The Sisters began immediately to forge important links with the outside world. Their early work, in addition to the education of young ladies at the Convent itself, was centred on Milton House in the Canongate, where they cared for the poor and needy children of Edinburgh. At the time of the Convent's Golden Jubilee in 1884 the Community built St. Ann's Seminary in Strathearn Road, which was used for a number of years as a school for the education of young

Catholic girls in Edinburgh. In more recent years a number of
additions have been made to the main building of the Convent
to maintain its position in the mainstream of Catholic
education in Scotland. Over the years the community also
took the opportunity of purchasing ground adjacent to the
Convent buildings to preserve its amenity and privacy from
the eyes of a changing neighbourhood. As early as 1858 they
acquired several acres of the Strathearn Parks on which
Strathearn Road is now built, and in 1878 they purchased
several acres to the north of the Whitehouse to ensure that the
tenement buildings of Thirlestane Road remained at a
respectable distance. One of the most ambitious schemes
which, unfortunately, was never implemented was Bishop
Gillis' concept of 'St. Margaret's Cathedral'. In 1849 it was the
Bishop's ardent desire to erect a cathedral and a college on the
ground previously purchased by him at Greenhill. He
employed Welby Pugin, the renowned ecclesiastical architect, to
draw plans and to consider the suitability of the site, but
unfortunately insufficient funds were forthcoming despite a
public exhibition of the plans in 1850. More than thirty years
later Mr. Pugin's plans for St. Margaret's Cathedral were
greatly admired at the Exhibition of Architectural Drawings in
Edinburgh in 1881, but by that time the residential villas of
Greenhill had been in existence for some time. The
opportunity had been lost for ever.

CHAPTER 7

Strathearn and Grange

Like the old professor of jurisprudence who maintained that one could not learn law by learning law, so too we cannot learn about Marchmont without learning something of the neighbouring districts. No district can be studied satisfactorily in isolation.

Strathearn and Grange are not strictly speaking part of Marchmont because they are outwith the area covered by the Warrender estates; nevertheless they are so closely associated with the modern district of Marchmont that some mention must be made of them. The story of the very ancient and historical district of Grange has been told many times, notably in *The Grange of St. Giles* by Mrs. J. Stewart Smith in 1898 and in *Historic South Edinburgh* by Charles J. Smith in 1978. An excellent publication with important emphasis on conservation in the Grange has recently been produced by the Grange Association. The present study is limited to that area where the boundaries of Grange and Marchmont converge.

Strathearn Road

Although Strathearn Road is now clearly part of the main thoroughfare between Church Hill and Salisbury, it was not always intended to be so. In the early days Grange Road was the main thoroughfare up to where the traffic lights at Kilgraston Road now are, but at that point a line of posts prevented heavy traffic from entering Strathearn Road. Instead of following what now appears to be the obvious route, the traffic turned down Kilgraston Road, along Hope Terrace and Clinton Road to emerge in Church Hill on the south side of St. Bennet's. The rather curious S bend in the roadway near St. Bennet's and the Iona Hotel was created in 1899 when the

City acquired one of the private houses and had it demolished to allow access from Strathearn Place into Church Hill. Before 1899 the old route was also used by the horse-drawn trams, but when the more direct route was created the opportunity was taken shortly thereafter to experiment with the very latest form of public transport — the cable car. Track was laid in Strathearn Road and Strathearn Place, despite protests from local residents who had until then enjoyed the benefit of living in a semi-rural locality. It was said that the line was specially designed to reduce the level of noise from the hauling gear, and that single track only was laid opposite one of the grandest houses, so that the cantankerous, but influential, owner could still have sufficient space to leave his horse and carriage outside his own gate. Such were the problems before the days of residents' parking zones.

In 1819 the lands of Whitehouse on which Strathearn Road was built passed to the ownership of Mrs. Ann Grant, widow of Francis Grant of Kilgraston in Perthshire. She sold the mansionhouse and part of the estate in 1834 to the Roman Catholic Community who founded St. Margaret's Convent in Whitehouse Loan. After the death of Mrs. Grant her trustees continued to feu out large sections of the estate for private development, particularly along the south side of Strathearn Road. However, on the north side, building was very sporadic, with the result that as late as 1900 much of the ground was still undeveloped. There was an orchard and kitchen garden for the convent, and where Strathfillan Road now stands there was a number of tennis courts used by the Whitehouse Lawn Tennis Club. On the same piece of ground in 1897 James S. Duncan the joiner of Thirlestane Lane built a curious little structure made out of railway sleepers to be used on a temporary basis as a stable and horse box, until the site was taken for the erection of tenement buildings. Just opposite at Nos. 10, 11 and 12 now occupied by the Army's Medical Reception Station was Strathearn College, managed for many years by the Principal, Miss Elizabeth Mitchell, under the direction of R.D. Graham, F.R.S.E., Principal of the

Fig 43.   The turrets and crowsteps of Mount Grange Hotel succumbed to the bulldozer in 1982.
Courtesy of the Cockburn Association

Edinburgh Southern Institute for the board and education of young ladies. The character of the south side of Strathearn Road near the junction with Kilgraston Road was greatly enhanced by the large walled gardens which, in the early days, extended down from the large houses in Hope Terrace. These were very long pieces of land which began to have a significant commercial value in the early 1900s. In 1915 the Post-Master General of the day, J.A. Pease, M.P. (Liberal), purchased part of the garden ground of No. 31 Hope Terrace, but owing to the severe financial restrictions imposed by the Great War the Post Office building was not completed until 1920. A few years later the small garage development was built in the ground of Mount Grange, and in 1930 W.T. Dunbar & Son Ltd. built the garage which is now occupied by Mr. Tom Farmer's ever-expanding empire of Kwik-Fit Euro Ltd. In more recent years the entire property at No. 35 Hope Terrace was demolished to permit the construction of Kilgraston

Court, and at the time of writing the Mount Grange property has also been demolished.

At the turn of the century Strathearn Road had not yet been visited by the entrepreneurs of the tenement building era, but 'progress' was just around the corner.

A Case for the Lords

On Christmas Eve in the year 1904 an urgent communication was delivered to the door of an elegant villa in Strathearn Road, occupied by the Murray household. Despite the time of year it did not bring tidings of great joy. It was, in fact, a copy of a petition to the Dean of Guild Court in Edinburgh, and it heralded the start of one of the longest and most bitterly fought arguments ever to arise in the development of Marchmont.

In 1855 the Trustees of Mrs. Ann Grant of Kilgraston had granted to David Murray a feu on the north side of Strathearn Road for the purpose of building a substantial villa. The villa was built, the extensive garden ground was laid out in a series of lawns and shrubberies, and there was a bowling green where Mr. Murray could relax in the evening after a busy day spent in the capacity of a senior Government official. He named his house St. Margaret's Tower in view of its proximity to the convent. A few years later, in 1858, the Grant Trustees feued a piece of ground next to Mr. Murray's property, to Dr. James Gillis who in turn disponed the property to St. Margaret's Convent. So that the new property owners could enjoy their amenity in perpetuity, a number of conditions were inserted in the feu charters.

By 1903 St. Margaret's Convent had acquired the superiority of their feu, and they began to feu out plots of land for building purposes at the north-east corner of Strathearn Road. An Edinburgh builder, George Alexander Wilson, acquired a number of building stances and submitted plans to the Dean of Guild Court for permission to erect tenement buildings. Unfortunately he did not make a good start because his first application was refused following an objection from property owners in Thirlestane Lane. He eventually appealed against the decision and won, but the setback was to prove a mere skirmish compared to what lay ahead. As he and the other builders pushed westward, towards St. Margaret's Tower, progress was suddenly halted. Murray's Trustees had viewed the plans for Strathfillan Road and had come to the conclusion that their idyllic setting would become less so if it were overlooked 'at a distance of 30′ by about sixty windows mostly from kitchen sculleries and closets with the usual accompaniments of external pipes, larders and clothes lines'. Noticeably hurt by the inference of inferior building, Mr. Wilson replied that 'the proposed tenements were to be superior flatted houses, fitted with electric light and with rents of £36–£48 thus ensuring a superior class of tenant'. It was soon obvious, however, that this was not a dispute which would be settled over the garden fence. The building site fell silent: the law offices bustled with activity, and Counsel began to study the old feu charters which had been drawn up half a century before. Eventually Murray's Trustees were advised to bring an action against both St. Margaret's Convent and the builder, Mr. Wilson. The case was heard on 17.11.1905 in the Court of Session before Lord Ardwall who found for the pursuers, effectively putting an end to the construction of Strathfillan Road. The excavated site lay under thick snow during the winter of 1905, but in the summer of 1906, on appeal to the Inner House of the Court of Session, the builder succeeded in convincing the court that the work should go ahead. Their Lordships had come to the conclusion that the old charters did not protect the Murrays' property in the way they had hoped. The builders now felt confident to return to the site, safe in the knowledge that they had in their favour a decision from Scotland's supreme court. But they were wrong. By virtue of the Appellate Jurisdiction Act 1876 the Murrays had one card left to play. The case came before the House of Lords on 13.5.1907, and in judgments considerably shorter than

Fig 44. St. Margaret's Tower, built in 1855 for David Murray.
Line drawing by Clare Hewitt

those normally emanating from this august tribunal, the Law
Lords dismissed the case. The Murrays had played their last
card and had lost.

St. Ann's Seminary

In Mr. and Mrs. Quested's newsagent's shop at No. 21
Strathearn Road there is a small area of ornate wall tiling, the
existence of which is not easily explained in a modern retail

Fig 45.   St. Ann's Seminary, opened in 1884 as a school for Catholic girls.
Line drawing by Clare Hewitt. See Fig 46

shop. The tiling was the idea of David Sutherland, who thought it would be both practical and ornamental in a corridor which gave access to a janitor's room, servants' quarters, and a children's cloakroom. The remainder of the ground floor consisted of two classrooms, a teacher's room and a parlour for receiving guests. At the far end of the hallway there was an elegant hardwood staircase, lit by a stained glass window, and leading to the upper floor on which there was a large assembly room, three other classrooms and two piano rooms. The foundation stone for this commodious building was laid on 20.9.1884 by Monsignor Smith on behalf of the Religious Ursulines of Jesus of St. Margaret's Convent for the purpose of providing sound religious education for Catholic girls in Edinburgh and its vicinity. The opening ceremony commenced with the words: 'Unless the Lord build the house, they labour in vain that build it'. Respect was paid to the good work of the Community, and in particular to the Right Rev. Dr. James Gillis, the founder of St. Margaret's Convent in 1834. In the foundation stone, with the inscription on parchment, was buried a copy of the Catholic Directory for the year 1884, a copy of the Gospel of St. John, the Prospectus of the Convent School and of the Seminary, a florin of Queen

Fig 46.   St. Ann's — 100 years on — only the upper storey is as it was. See
Fig 45.

Courtesy of the Royal Bank of Scotland

Victoria of 1883, and a medal of Pope Leo XIII. In this way
there came into being the much needed St. Ann's Seminary or
School Villa, which was built to overcome the acute problem
of accommodation at their old premises in Castle Terrace.

   The building of St. Ann's is still very much in existence,
though greatly altered by a succession of different owners and
different usage. Today the Royal Bank operates from what
were two classrooms, Mr. and Mrs. Quested sell stationery
from the parlour, White's do their cleaning in the cloakroom,
the upper floor is converted into comfortable living
accommodation, and the playground has been given over to
Hamilton the jeweller, W.D. McGregor the grocer and the
Trustee Savings Bank. Fortunately, owing to the co-operation
of the various shopkeepers, the banks, and Sister St. Ignatius
Edwards of St. Margaret's Convent, it has been possible for
Clare Hewitt to produce an accurate drawing of how St.

Ann's would have looked in 1884, creating an interesting contrast with the photograph commissioned by the Royal Bank of Scotland in 1983.

Marchmont St. Giles Church

The spire and clock of Marchmont St. Giles Church in Kilgraston Road is perhaps the most prominent landmark in the district. In the old days before it was fashionable for young children to have the luxury of a wrist watch, it was common for keen young eyes to read the time on the clock from as far away as the Blackford Hill and hopefully make it home in time to be at the table with the rest of the family. In those days, of course, the name Marchmont St. Giles was unheard of, or at any rate in relation to that particular church.

Although the church now draws a large part of its congregation from the district of Marchmont, it was actually built to accommodate the residents of the Grange and Whitehouse before the Marchmont tenements had been thought of. The earliest recorded meeting was on 21.11.1867 at 21 Findhorn Place, when a number of residents discussed the erection of a parish church in the district. In January of the following year more definite plans were implemented and a fund was started for the construction of a stone church, to plans drawn by Robert Morham, the architect. It was originally built as the Robertson Memorial Church in memory of the Rev. Dr. James Robertson, Professor of Ecclesiastical History in the University of Edinburgh and Convener of the Endowment Committee of the Church of Scotland, but it was later named the Grange Parish Church. It was opened for worship on 1.10.1871, although for some months before that the congregation had used a temporary iron church which lay between the site of the permanent church and Beaufort Road. Services taken by the first minister, Rev. W.L. Riach, were very much different from what we are accustomed to today. There was no organ, and there were no hymns either, despite

Fig 47.   Marchmont St. Giles Church in the noonday sun.
Photograph by Malcolm Liddle

the fact that Scotland's foremost hymn writer, Rev. Horatius Bonar, lived and worked within a few hundred yards of Kilgraston Road. The congregation stood for prayer, sat for singing of psalms and paraphrases, and no doubt slept for part

H

of the very lengthy and commanding sermons. In what must rank as one of the most revealing stories of human 'weakness', one of the staunchest members of the congregation admitted to the minister that her only way of enduring the full impact of the early sermons was to gaze at the stained glass window depicting the wise men's gift of gold and imagine how best she would spend it if it were all hers!

Over the years the congregation grew in strength and numbers, eventually gaining a larger membership than the neighbouring Free Church at the top of Chalmers Crescent, but in the 1930s that trend was reversed by the erection of the new Reid Memorial Church at Blackford Station. Nevertheless the Grange Parish Church operated under a succession of prominent clergymen and celebrated its centenary in October 1971 with a number of special services and meetings. An interesting time capsule was placed within the church building with objects of the time to be opened in the year 2071. The lead casket contained newspapers of the day, coins, *Life and Work* magazine for October 1971, and other items pertaining to the church.

In 1972 Grange Church entered into an Act of Union with Warrender Church and West St. Giles Church to form the new Marchmont St. Giles congregation. In doing so the new church assumed the status of a burgh church in continuation of that ancient right previously held by West St. Giles. The new congregation has therefore a most ancient and interesting history to conserve. Its ancestry can be traced through West St. Giles to the year 1699, and through Warrender Church to the little iron church which was erected in Warrender Park Road, in 1885, as an offshoot to the Barclay Free Church of Edinburgh.

Grange Cemetery

In 1845 a group of Edinburgh businessmen purchased an old property in Causewayside, with a view to having it demolished. Little is known about the property other than that it was close to what was described on the early maps as Baxter's Feu, to the west of the High Road between Edinburgh and Liberton. In terms of modern day street names, the property stood at the foot of Grange Road near the junction with Causewayside. The men involved in the purchase were the directors of the Edinburgh Southern Cemetery Company who had acquired several acres of ground on the Grange estates with the intention of laying out what was to become Grange Cemetery. Before these days even the earliest villas of the Grange had not yet been constructed, and the only main places of habitation were Grange House and Grange Farm. Farmland stretched from Sheens Loan (now Sciennes Road) in the north to Grange Loan in the south. The streets of Kilgraston Road and Strathearn Road had not yet been constructed, and therefore the only means of access to the new cemetery was along the rough track laid from the Causewayside entrance. From such humble beginnings there developed Grange Road, now one of the main roads through the district, which at one time belonged to the Dick-Lauder family. Towards the end of his life Sir Thomas Dick-Lauder described the new cemetery designed by the architect David Bryce in these words:

> One large space is now being laid out in the most beautiful manner with shrubberies and walks as the Great Southern Cemetery, everything being done that refined taste in architecture or gardening can accomplish to remove those dark and chilling associations which have hitherto made us behold with shuddering disquiet that grave which ought to be so full of attraction for the weary Christian.

The wearied Christian himself died on 29.5.1848 and was buried in Grange Cemetery on the highest point of ground and nearest to Grange House, for many years the home of the Dick-Lauder family. The funeral cortege consisting of a large hearse preceded by ushers, the family carriage and twenty-two mourning and private carriages, left Grange House at half-past-

Fig 48.　Grange Cemetery with Arthur's Seat and Salisbury Crags in the background.

Photograph by A.C. Robson

two on a Tuesday afternoon and reached the cemetery gates by way of Grange Loan, Causewayside, and Grange Road. Several hundred spectators gathered at the cemetery to witness the funeral procession and the burial.

Some years later in 1865, when part of the district had been feued for private houses, a proposal was put forward for the construction of another approach to the cemetery, this time from the north. The idea was to continue the Middle Meadow Walk in a southerly direction along the line of what is now Argyle Place and Chalmers Crescent to its junction with Palmerston Road. At that point the Walk was to open out into a crescent immediately opposite the Grange Cemetery, but no part of these proposals was ever implemented.

The cemetery is the final resting place of many eminent Edinburgh citizens, including Thomas Guthrie, Thomas Chalmers, Thomas Dick-Lauder, and the Sisters Ursulines of Jesus of St. Margaret's Convent. In 1924 the Cemetery Company took the unusual step of purchasing the two large

Fig 49. A palm, in stone, shades the tomb of the Stuart family in Grange Cemetery.

Photograph by A.C. Robson

detached properties, Nos. 3 and 5 Kilgraston Road, just to the south of Marchmont St. Giles Church, as an extension to the cemetery. The houses were demolished, the gates and pillars removed, and the front walls were heightened to form the west boundary of the cemetery.

In 1976 Edinburgh District Council took over responsibility for Grange Cemetery, which has been kept in much better condition than many other old burial grounds in the City. It has, however, suffered considerable damage by vandalism on more than one occasion in recent years.

St. Catherine's Argyle Church

When the tenement buildings of Marchmont were being built in the late nineteenth century a number of churches were anxious to establish congregations in the district. There was Warrender Park Church in 1885, West St. Giles Church in 1883, Argyle Place Church in 1877, and the Robertson Memorial Church in 1871. Before these churches were ever considered, or indeed needed, there was a thriving congregation in the Grange under the name of the Chalmers Memorial Free Church. In the 1850s land belonging to Sir John Dick-Lauder was being feued out for the building of villa properties, although the new district was still in its infancy. There was a growing population in the area between Grange Loan and Grange Road but, to the north, Hatton Place, Chalmers Crescent and Palmerston Road had not yet been built. There were, however, a sufficient number of people keen to start a new Free Church congregation, if possible on a site about midway between the existing Free Churches of Barclay in the west and Newington in the east. By 1862 Clare Hall in Causewayside had been rented for regular Sunday worship, and in the following year Rev. Prof. Smeaton, D.D. moved into the district and held Sunday services for a while at his home in Mansionhouse Road. In 1865 the new congregation received the sanction of the Presbytery, a site was secured for the new church on the corner of Chalmers Crescent and Grange Road, and the foundation stone was laid on 13.10.1865 by Lord Kintore. The official name given to the church was the Chalmers Memorial Free Church, but under its first minister, Rev. Dr. Horatius Bonar, it was generally known as the Grange Free Church. Its first Communion Roll in October 1866 was 61, which had risen to 170 by February 1867. There was a setback in 1883 when a number of members and office-

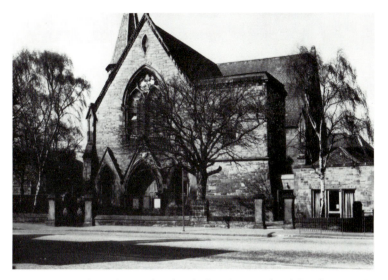

Fig 50. St. Catherine's Argyle Church showing, on the right, the extension opened in 1982.

Photograph by A.C. Robson

bearers left the church on account of the introduction of the *Free Church Hymn Book*. But by 1888 the congregation had obviously made up any losses, as the Communion Roll was then 805.

In 1900, following the Union of the Free Church with the United Presbyterian Church, Grange Free Church became Grange United Free Church. In 1929, at the historic Union between the United Free Church and the old Established Church, the congregation took its place in the new Church of Scotland under the attractive name St. Catherine's in Grange, recalling the dedication of the pre-Reformation convent nearby to St. Catherine of Siena.

The history of any church, of course, can never stand still, or at any rate not for long. Although St. Catherine's in Grange continued to serve the community for many years after 1929, there came a time in the late 1960s when the climate in church affairs was considered favourable for a possible union between the congregation of St. Catherine's and the

Fig 51. In the roll of Disruption Worthies the first place belongs by universal consent to Thomas Chalmers.

Photograph from Disruption Worthies 1876

congregation of Argyle Place Church. By May 1968 a basis of union had been worked out and approved, it being decided that the Argyle Place Church would be used as the place of worship and that the St. Catherine's building would be used for additional accommodation. Following the fire which destroyed Argyle Place Church in 1974, it was decided that St. Catherine's should once again become the place of worship for the congregation. An extension was built alongside the church with access from Lovers' Loan and opened in February 1982. The united congregation under the name St. Catherine's Argyle has overcome its difficulties and faces the future with renewed vigour.

The Real St. Trinnean's

When Alastair Sim died in 1976, Edinburgh lost another of her sons of fame, and the world lost one of its most accomplished actors, of whom it was said that there was not a single thought, however fleeting, which could not be conveyed by his expressive countenance. That his body could produce what his mind was thinking was superbly demonstrated in his role as the headmistress in *The Belles of St. Trinians*, produced in 1954 by Frank Launder and Sidney Gilliat. Although Alastair Sim had been absent from Edinburgh for some years prior to the making of the film, he would be well aware that the growing legend of St. Trinians had a much more sombre origin in the town of his boyhood. In Edinburgh in the 1950s there were many sophisticated young ladies whose moments of embarrassment would have been far fewer had it not been for the creative talents of Ronald Searle, the cartoonist. Even today, the announcement that St. Trinnean's School did exist tends to be met with either stunned silence or hearty laughter.

The real St. Trinnean's School, for boarding and day pupils, began life in 1922 at No. 10 Palmerston Road under its headmistress, Miss C. Fraser Lee, whose single-minded ability earned her the reputation of being 'a committee of one'. Her resolve did not, however, mean that she was in any way narrow-minded. In fact, in relation to the educational philosophy of the day her concept of the Dalton Plan was revolutionary, and attracted a great deal of attention, and criticism. It was said by her critics that it was 'the school where they do what they like', but although there was considerable emphasis on freedom, the general atmosphere of the school was the very opposite of Searle's cartoons. At no time did they ever stab a mistress or string her up to the branch of a tree! Instead, the school was divided into four Senior Houses, Whithorn, Monenn, Clagrinnie and Kilninian whose duty it was to elect two girls each as representatives for the Senate presided over by the Head Girl. The Senate drew up Rules of Convenience and Danger Rules and took an active part in the maintenance of self-discipline. The Dalton system allowed a certain degree of freedom in arranging study time. After roll call at 9 a.m. the girls went to the various Study Rooms of their choice and were free to move from one subject to another during the course of the morning. In order to maintain control, each pupil was provided with sufficient work for a month, arranged into weeks, with a calendar on which she marked the time given to each subject. Each week's assignment was checked by the House Mistress to ensure that an adequate time had been allotted to each subject, and if there was time left over this was taken up by the system of Opportunity Work, preferably devoted to the girl's weakest subject. In this way Miss Lee maintained that she developed the pupils' sense of responsibility and prepared them more adequately for the freedom which they would find in the Colleges and the Universities.

It was probably this concept of freedom which was the common denominator between Miss Fraser Lee's St. Trinnean's and the St. Trinians of the cartoon world. Although Miss Lee and Ronald Searle never met, they were both well aware of where their paths had crossed.

In the little town of Kirkcudbright there has been for many years a thriving community of artists drawn to the exceptional clarity of light for which the surrounding countryside is so well known. It was not, however, the clarity of light which brought Ronald Searle to Kirkcudbright: it was the Royal Engineers, and the only brushes provided were those with which to shine his boots, because the year was 1941 and he was serving with H.M. Forces as Sapper Searle. Befriended by the Johnston family, who were living there as evacuees, he demonstrated, by way of a domestic joke, his idea of the school attended by the two daughters of the Johnston family. The school was St. Trinnean's in Edinburgh. Although the cartoon was sent to *Lilliput* in July 1941, and published, nothing more was heard of Searle's work until 1946, after he was eventually released from a Japanese prisoner-of-war camp. But even in these hideous conditions his talents could not be hidden. On odd scraps of paper he put together some of his most interesting cartoons, many of which reflected the violent nature of his surroundings whilst held prisoner. When he returned to Britain at the end of the war, *Lilliput* produced his cartoons and brought St. Trinians to the attention of the world.

St. Trinnean's in Edinburgh remained at Palmerston Road only until 1925, when it removed to St. Leonard's House in Dalkeith Road. At the outbreak of War in 1939 the school was evacuated to Gala House in Galashiels, but owing to lack of accommodation and the retirement of the headmistress, the school closed in September 1946. The memory of the blue seas and golden sands of Iona which gave their colours to the school faded from the streets of Galashiels and Edinburgh, but the motto *Solus Agus Sonas* — Light and Joy — shone from the 'spartan daughter of the Highlands', Miss C. Fraser Lee, all of her long and eventful life.

No. 9 Palmerston Road

Within a hundred yards of the old St. Trinnean's School, but on the other side of Palmerston Road, there is an elegant property which has now been skilfully divided into separate dwellings without any obvious interference with the external appearance of the house. In recent years, a not unusual domestic situation arose which, unknown to the participants at the time, created an interesting historical coincidence. One of the self-contained dwellings had been taken by two young Edinburgh girls who made it the centre of their busy lives, until one of them emigrated to Canada. When she married in Canada a few years later, the other girl went out to be present at the ceremony and to join in the celebrations. In a curious way, the Canadian connection was repeating itself, albeit for a social purpose far removed from the days when the house was built in 1868.

In that year the house at No. 9 was occupied by the Rev.

William G. Blaikie, D.D., who had just been elected by the
General Assembly as Professor of Apologetics and Pastoral
Theology in New College, Edinburgh. He moved to
Palmerston Road with his wife and large family after having
been minister at Pilrig Church for some years. Both Rev.
William G. Blaikie and his wife had already earned themselves
a considerable reputation in helping the poor in the City of
Edinburgh before they came under the influence of work
being done by Miss Annie Macpherson in London. Miss
Macpherson engaged in what was described as the
matchmaking industry of the metropolis. This entailed
'emigrating' children from the slums of provincial cities to
various parts of Canada, where young settlers either had no
children of their own or required young domestic staff. After
one of their visits to Miss Macpherson's London organisation,
the Blaikies returned to Edinburgh 'with the conviction that
here was a valuable outlet for the disposal of multitudes of
children in our city who would otherwise be brought up in
vice, misery and degradation'. When the Society for
Improving the Condition of the Poor refused to get involved
in any scheme which involved sending children out of the
country, the Blaikies decided to go it alone, in the belief that
extreme evils required extreme remedies. They set up a house
in Carlung Place (now part of Sciennes Road) and later in
Lauriston Lane as Mrs. Blaikie's Orphan and Emigration
Home. Business was brisk, there being no shortage of children
living in appalling conditions in the high tenements of the Old
Town, and who, in the opinion of the City Missionaries,
would benefit enormously from a new life across the water.
They were brought to Mrs. Blaikie, and provided the child
was well enough for the journey and provided the parents did
not sustain their objection, arrangements were made for
emigration. She did not, of course, just send the children
abroad without caring what happened to them. She had
already made elaborate plans for them to be received into
good Christian families, and she made frequent trips abroad to
ensure that the children were properly cared for. No one,

however, ever pretended that the scheme did not have certain disadvantages, chiefly associated with that bond which exists between any child and its parents, however disreputable the parents may be. The problem had the habit of manifesting itself at a time when it was least expected. At one difficult scene at the platform of the Caledonian Railway there was a furore at which one drunken woman, intent on getting back her little girl, was heard to say, 'It's that wuman wi' the white shawl that's at the bottom o' it a'. It oughtn't tae be alloo'd.'

But alloo'd it was, for several years, and not without good reason, as can be seen from any one of many case studies which were all too frequent in Edinburgh at that time:

> Mother dead. Father a drunkard. The children were found in a filthy room; no fire, no furniture, nothing in the room but a few bricks for a pillow; the father lying in the corner on a few straws with a coal sack over him. The children had a little bread and butter and a jug of water on the dirty floor and a piece of candle on the top of the loaf.

The Blaikies maintained the Home for several years until their health and age made it difficult for them to continue, but by that time they could see the light at the end of the tunnel, however dimly. By 1884 a formal organisation had been set up in the hope of preventing the situations arising which had made it so necessary for Mrs. Blaikie to send the children away from their native land. In 1984 the Royal Society for the Prevention of Cruelty to Children will celebrate its centenary.

CHAPTER 8

Roseneath and Argyle

There are few areas in the district of Marchmont which are more interesting than that which is now occupied by the streets of Roseneath and Argyle. According to *Bartholomew's Chronological Map of Edinburgh,* there were a number of inhabited dwellings in Roseneath as early as 1622, and no doubt before that date there were houses of more humble construction. The line of what is now Melville Drive formed the southern edge of the Borough Loch or South Loch which served as the source of water supply for Edinburgh before the Comiston Springs were piped in 1676. In those days the loch occupied most of the ground which now forms the Meadows and was the natural breeding ground of many birds and wild fowl which frequented the long grasses on the southern bank. It was this tranquil scene which incurred the wrath of the authorities sitting up in the Auld Toon just a mile or so to the north. There had developed the practice among the many poor women of neighbouring districts to cut the 'gyrs' or tall grasses to feed their cattle, but the extent to which this was being done had increased so much that there was a real risk to wild life around the loch. In an attempt to curtail the activities of the gyrs women, an order was issued by the Town making the cutting of the grass an offence 'that na gyrs women nor utheris pas within the South Loch to cheir the gyrs thairof, hary the burd nestis, tak away the eggis of the saming befae Midsummer next under the payne of skurgein'. The authorities had great difficulty in curtailing this ancient custom, but eventually the Loch was drained between 1722 and about 1740, opening the way for the laying out of the Meadows as we know them today. However, the success of the scheme was by no means immediate, if the account in the *New Picture of Edinburgh* in 1806 is anything to go by:

The whole Meadows is about half a league in circumference; but it were to be wished that it had been much better drained at the beginning in order to prevent the pernicious effects of stagnant waters which during the heat of the summer must emit a very offensive smell and contaminate the atmosphere with noxious effluvia. For these reasons the pleasure of the walk is not only diminished but the seeds of disease may be inhaled with every breath. It is to be hoped however that these evils will be remedied in due time as the magistrates have begun to use every laudable exertion for the accomplishment of that object.

The draining of the Loch no doubt served as an impetus to the development of the inhabited area along the south bank which had previously been cut off from the City of Edinburgh by the expanse of water and marshland. Despite greatly improved communication, the area around Roseneath remained a sleepy little community for some time thereafter. The habit had grown up of describing the addresses of houses in the area as 'lying at the back of the Meadows', but later two place names emerged which have, in turn, fallen into disuse. There was the district of Westerhall, and there was the district of New Campbeltown. Whilst they were not separated in any geographical sense, their ultimate destiny has dictated that they be treated separately now.

Westerhall

Today it is possible to see what was Westerhall in something less than ten minutes by walking round the block of tenement buildings bounded by Roseneath Street, Argyle Place, Roseneath Terrace and Roseneath Place. In these few acres there was, until less than a hundred years ago, a thriving community of merchants and intellectuals whose mode of life was very different to that of the present-day flat-dwellers. In the late 1870s the construction of Warrender Park Road was just commencing and there was still a very marked division in the form of a high stone wall between the lands belonging to

Sir George Warrender and the lands on which Westerhall stood. That boundary can still be seen today along the line of the trees and the old stone wall and railings which divide the lower half of Marchmont Crescent from Roseneath Place. At one time that same wall turned eastwards at the police box and telephone box and ran along to the top of Argyle Place. The present confusion of having one street with a different name on each side is accounted for by the fact that the south side (Warrender Park Road) was built in 1878 on land belonging to Sir George Warrender and the north side (Roseneath Street) was built in 1897 after the boundary wall had been removed and after the old houses of Westerhall had been demolished.

Originally Westerhall consisted of half a dozen fairly substantial houses with a number of lodges, outbuildings, and stables. Most of the houses had very extensive garden ground laid out with ornamental lawns and shrubberies around which were laid elegant paths and terraces. The grandest of these was Argyle Park, a substantial villa which stood in extensive grounds on the site of what is now the tenement buildings of Argyle Place. This house was for long the residence of a succession of successful merchants in the City and latterly was taken over by the Misses Jamieson who used it as a boarding school for young ladies.

Its greatest claim to fame must, however, be its undoubted connection with the notorious *Beacon* newspaper which circulated in Edinburgh for a few months in 1821. When Duncan Stevenson, Deputy Lieutenant and Justice of the Peace for the County of Argyll, left his father's troubled Glenfeochan Estate near Oban in 1816, he set up residence at No. 16 Meadow Place, but when he moved to the much grander property at Argyle Park in 1820, it heralded the start of one of Scotland's bitterest political wrangles of the time. Duncan Stevenson had been a reasonably successful printer in Edinburgh for some years before he became involved in the printing and publishing of the Tory-sponsored *Beacon*, the prospectus for which claimed that it would aspire to a place in the public favour which in the city was wholly unoccupied.

When the paper went on to claim to be the Champion of Civil Rights and to accuse the leaders of society of having acquired popularity by the basest means and to have used it for the vilest purposes, it was obviously set on a collision course with its political opponents, the Whigs. The *Beacon* was actually founded by a group of prominent Tories, including Sir Walter Scott, who each subscribed £100, but they soon became disillusioned and worried by the tenor of the editorials. These had been left in the hands of young and inexperienced journalists who were not long in bringing the newspaper into one scandal after another. Whilst Scott had no love of the Whigs, he became increasingly worried by the methods used by the paper, which continued to launch scurrilous attacks upon leading members of society. The 'slang whanging vocation' of the editors was, however, to contribute to their eventual downfall, though not before a great deal of harm had been done. One of the first people to be on the receiving end of the *Beacon*'s quest for social justice was James Stuart of Dunearn. Early in 1821 Stuart discovered that what he considered to be libellous statements were being circulated by the *Beacon,* but on confronting Duncan Stevenson he was told that he, Stevenson, was merely the printer and had no control over the editorial policy of the newspaper. Dissatisfied with the explanation, and exasperated by his inability to locate the offending pen, Stuart decided on an attack of his own. On sighting his adversary one day in Parliament Square, he struck Stevenson several times with a horsewhip, whereupon Stevenson retaliated by lashing out with a bamboo walking-stick. Such undignified behaviour on the streets of Edinburgh did not escape the attention of the Sheriff, and did nothing to resolve the growing acrimony between the two men. The *Beacon* resorted to the only weapon available to it by stepping up coverage of the Stuart affair and printing disparaging poems about the opposition. Meantime even Sir Walter Scott was being drawn into the web and had narrowly missed being challenged to a duel by one James Gibson who had wrongly assumed that Sir Walter had also penned libellous statements in

J

the *Beacon*. By then, enough was enough: the original founders issued a joint statement that Scott was not involved; they withdrew their financial support, and the newspaper closed in September 1821 without having completed even a full year'of publication. Had the story ended there, it could have been written off as a foolish episode, but instead it was destined to become a tragedy. Although the *Beacon* was dead, its seditious seed had cloned another of the same, the *Sentinel,* and the whole sordid affair was opened up again. One of the eminent Tory contributors to the *Beacon* had been Sir Alexander Boswell of Auchinleck (son of Johnson's biographer), whose wit and caustic humour had always been used to advantage against his political opponents. One of the contributions to the new *Sentinel* in Glasgow again contained derogatory and untrue statements about James Stuart of Dunearn, and was traced to Boswell. Stuart challenged Boswell to a duel which took place on 26.3.1822 at Auchertool in Fife, as a result of which Boswell received a neck wound from which he died the following day. Stuart was charged with murder but was acquitted.

The *Beacon* had, of course, ceased to shed any light on the political scene in Edinburgh by the late 1870s, when the garden ground of Argyle Park was subdivided into building stances, and the old villa later demolished. The earliest tenement development was at the north end around 1873 when several small buildings were demolished to make way for the construction of Argyle Park Terrace. Having been built at a time when the area of authority of the Dean of Guild Court did not extend as far as Marchmont, there is unfortunately no immediate information available now as to the identity of the builder or the architect. However, high up on the face of the building there is a sculptured panel with a date 1873 and what appear to be the entwined initials ABC. By a cruel irony the initials are the only ones in Marchmont which have so far escaped positive identification, although the evidence might suggest 'Argyle Building Company' as a possible solution. One thing is, however, certain. Had the problem arisen in 1875, the

Fig 52. No. 16 Meadow Place, one-time home of Duncan Stevenson of the notorious *Beacon* newspaper.

Line drawing by Clare Hewitt

solution would surely have been elementary because in that year the adjacent turreted top flat dwelling (No. 2 Argyle Park Terrace) was inhabited by Arthur Conan Doyle. Following an intense and exhaustive study of the Edinburgh roots of Sherlock Holmes, a most interesting and persuasive argument has been put forward by Owen Dudley Edwards in support of his theory that many of the locations in the Sherlock Holmes stories were based on Doyle's recollections of Edinburgh rather than his knowledge of London. In *The Quest for Sherlock*

Holmes, Mr. Edwards refers to the scene in 'The Beryl Coronet' in which Watson observes from a bow window the eccentric approach of the banker Alexander Holder, he suggests the similarity between it and the view of the snow-covered Meadows which Doyle would have had from his own bow window at Argyle Park Terrace. Although Conan Doyle's story is based on 221B Baker Street, London, Sherlockologists have always been puzzled by the fact that Baker Street does not have any bow windows. On the other hand No. 2 Argyle Park Terrace certainly has a most interesting corbelled turret with a bow window overlooking the new flats at Argyle Park House.

The demise of Argyle Park Villa in the 1870s must have been a salutary reminder to the other owners of Westerhall that their idyllic surroundings were not going to last forever. The plans for the Warrender estate nearby were well advanced, tenement buildings had sprung up in Argyle Park Terrace and Marchmont Crescent, and the proposed development on the Argyle Park site meant that the amenity of a number of villa properties would be completely spoiled. The house which was most vulnerable was Warrender Lodge immediately to the west of Argyle Park and occupying the site of what is now the centre of the tenements in Roseneath Street. When the demolition men moved in to remove the stone and lime and to lay main drains across the lawns, they probably thought little of the memory of James Ballantine who had made Warrender Lodge the centre of his long and useful life. A glass stainer by profession, he was employed by the Royal Commissioners on the Fine Arts to execute the stained glass windows for the House of Lords at Westminster. Not only was he master of his profession, but he also showed considerable skill as an author with *The Gaberlunzie's Wallet* in 1843 and *The Miller of Deanhaugh* in 1845, and as a song writer with 'Ilka blade o' grass keps its ain drap o' dew'. When he died in 1877 there were, no doubt, a few blades of grass on the lawns at Warrender Lodge which would soon never see another drop of dew. Before the end of the century the house had been demolished, the tenements had been built in Roseneath Street, and back-green washing poles stood where 'croquet once was played'.

In addition to the two biggest houses already mentioned, there were three dwellings which all took their name from the district of Westerhall. There was Westerhall Lodge just to the west of Warrender Lodge; Westerhall Cottage on the corner of what is now Roseneath Street and Roseneath Place; and Westerhall Villa in Roseneath Place just before the entrance to Roseneath Terrace. In those days, of course, the streets were not the same as they are today. Roseneath Street was called Westerhall and looked out over the green fields of the Warrender Estate. What is now Roseneath Place was formerly referred to as Warrender's Lane and gave access to a very short narrow lane which was later widened to create Roseneath Terrace. The curious thing about Westerhall Villa was that although it had an extensive frontage to Warrender's Lane, entry to it was gained from the small lane which also gave access to a very old property called Yew Tree House. This dwelling stood at the west end of Roseneath Terrace and was bought and demolished in 1884 by one of Marchmont's speculative builders of the day, Mr. John Oliver.

Over the years many eminent citizens of Edinburgh resided at Westerhall, including D.I. Robertson the City Chamberlain and Alexander Christie, R.S.A., the renowned historical and portrait painter who lived at Westerhall Lodge in 1858. Like many educated men of his day, Christie started life as a law apprentice, but it was not long before he decided to devote himself to the world of art. In his formative years he studied under Sir William Allan and followed the tradition as a painter of historical subjects. Many of his subjects were taken from the novels of Sir Walter Scott, the life of Mary Queen of Scots and the Jacobite Rebellion.

In the last decade of Westerhall's existence, Mr. William Thorburn, the well-known family grocer, lived at Westerhall Villa, and Mr. William Purves, the cabinetmaker and funeral director, began his business in 1888 in premises which had been constructed a few years previously in the grounds of Westerhall Villa.

But these times have all gone, and the buildings with them. Of Westerhall nothing remains: not even a single stone. All fell victim to the speculative builder who was active in and around Roseneath about a hundred years ago. In fairness to the builders, however, it must be said that in the years immediately prior to the building of the tenements many of the villa owners had moved out, leaving the houses let to tenants, and generally the area was becoming less attractive. The building programme around the turn of the century transformed the district and gave rise to the solid facades of the Scottish tenement buildings as we know them today.

New Campbeltown

Although the demise of Westerhall was all but total, the neighbouring area of New Campbeltown escaped at least some of the 'advantages' of progress. Its geographical limits are not easy to determine but can be taken to include the houses of what is now known as Meadow Place.

Perhaps the best-known section of Meadow Place is that row of very old terraced houses built in 1805 which sit at the back of long narrow gardens fronting Melville Drive. These are among the oldest houses in the area, many of which are still in private occupation, No. 6 being for long the residence of David Irving, LL.D., librarian to the Faculty of Advocates and author of *The Lives of the Scotish Poets*. David Irving, a brilliant intellectual and contributor to the *Encyclopaedia Britannica,* insisted that the word was 'Scotish' with one 't' and that 'Scottish', although in more general use, was actually a corruption.

Towards the end of the 1870s the Warrender estate was undergoing extensive change, with the earliest of the tenements being built nearby in Marchmont Crescent. Given this changing scene, it is hardly surprising that New Campbeltown was also affected. By 1878 a number of properties at the west end of Meadow Place had been demolished to permit the building of the range of tenements that face Marchmont Road, but it was John Oliver who was destined to make the greatest changes. Having already completed a number of dwellings in Marchmont Crescent, he then turned his attention to the old houses which stood in large gardens on the New Campbeltown side of the Warrender boundary. In 1884 he acquired and demolished Yew Tree House, and in the following year he acquired the property opposite (No. 17 Meadow Place) to build Nos. 29, 31 and 33 Roseneath Terrace. No doubt encouraged by the success of these ventures, he then put forward elaborate plans for the demolition and redevelopment of No. 16 Meadow Place, built many years previously on the site of another house which had been destroyed by fire in 1794. However, the opposition to his plans was so intense that he was forced to make considerable compromises before winning the approval of the Dean of Guild Court. His original idea was to build a tenement on the site of the old house, with a pend giving access to a smithy, and sheds to be used in connection with his business. The neighbours were not amused. Jessie Proudfoot, the proprietor of No. 20, wrote to the Dean of Guild and pointed out that the smoke from the chimneys would be intolerable and that the inhabitants of the surrounding properties should not be required to put up with the early morning noise from the smithy's anvil. Her pleas were heard. Mr. Oliver re-submitted his plans for the tenement but omitted the pend, the workshops, and the smithy. Not only was the decision welcomed by the neighbouring property owners, but it was also instrumental in creating another interesting chapter in the history of Roseneath.

In 1854 was born Patrick W. Adam, the son of an Edinburgh lawyer. Instead of following in the family tradition, Patrick decided to follow his love of art and become a student at the Royal Scottish Academy, where he came under the influence of the leading Scottish painters of the day. He was elected an Associate of the Academy in 1883 and within a few years was sufficiently established to have a studio built for himself in the district of New Campbeltown. It was at this studio that Patrick Adam painted his series of Venetian pictures in 1889, amongst which were 'The Ducal Palace' and the 'Santa Maria della Salute', but it is generally considered that his most striking work was a number of winter landscapes completed about 1896. He gained the distinction of R.S.A. in 1897.

Although it is almost a century since Patrick Adam's studio was built, it has been used continuously over the years by several members of the art world, most notable amongst whom was Eric Schilsky, the sculptor. Eric Schilsky was born in Southampton on 22.10.1898 into a musical family, his father being Charles Schilsky, the famous violinist and leader of the originator of the Proms, Henry Wood's, Queen's Hall Orchestra, but it was in the world of art that Eric made his impact. His introduction to the study of art began when he was at school in Geneva, but he was to arrive on a much higher plane when he studied sculpture under Harvard Thomas at the Slade in London. He came to Edinburgh in 1945 as Head of the School of Sculpture at the Edinburgh College of Art, a post which he held until his retirement in 1969. In 1946 he married Victorine Foot the painter, both artists working at the studio for many years until his death in 1974. The studio was converted in 1951 by the architect Alan Reiach to include residential accommodation. Since her husband's death, Victorine Foot has continued her work, maintaining all the best traditions of a studio which will celebrate its centenary within the next few years.

During his long lifetime Schilsky received many honours, being elected A.R.S.A. in 1952, and an Academician in 1956. The Royal Academy, London also elected him an Associate in 1957, and an Academician in 1968. He will probably be best remembered for a special quality which he brought to the art of sculpture and which is probably best described in his own words: 'a sensitive artist can make a good figure with little

Fig 53. Victorine Foot in the studio among her late husband's sculpture.
Courtesy of Victorine Foot (Mrs. Schilsky)

knowledge of anatomy but if he is not first an artist, no amount of anatomical knowledge will help him'.

The district, then, has certainly been the home of a number of very eminent artists — Christie, Adam, and Schilsky — but it has been left to the fairer sex to maintain these traditions in the present day. Within a few yards of one another, in the very heart of what was New Campbeltown, three very talented artists live and work, Victorine Foot, Clare Hewitt and Sheila Cant.

The story of New Campbeltown could never be complete without tracing the origins of one last quotation:

> For the health of my wife and children I have taken the little country house at which you visited my uncle Dr. B. who, having lost his wife, is gone to live with his son. We took possession of our villa about a week ago. We have a garden of three-quarters of an acre, well stocked with fruit-trees and flowers. I now write to you in a little study from the window of which I see around me a verdant grove and beyond it the lofty mountain called Arthur's Seat.

Fig 54.   Boswell's House, showing the alterations done in 1881.
Courtesy of Edinburgh City Libraries

But for the rather quaint phraseology, the message could have been written yesterday by someone spending an enjoyable summer holiday at a country resort. In fact, it was penned on 9th June 1777 by James Boswell, and the recipient of the letter was none other than the celebrated Dr. Johnson. Thanks to detailed research by the late W. Forbes Gray, himself an eminent authority on matters relating to Edinburgh, it has been established that the house owned by Dr. Boswell and at which both James Boswell and Dr. Johnson visited, is No. 15a Meadow Place. The house is still in existence, although greatly altered and extended in 1881 to form two separate houses. At the time of these alterations a number of very interesting

papers relating to Dr. Boswell's occupation of the house were
found behind a wall cupboard, these items apparently having
lain undisturbed for more than a century.

Sylvan House

Before we leave Westerhall and New Campbeltown, there is
one other property which deserves special mention but which
would require much more detailed research before yielding the
secrets of yesteryear. Sylvan House, now entered by a small
lane off Sylvan Place, clearly belongs to a period much earlier
than the houses which surround it. It is generally considered to
be the property originally known as 'William's Hut' erected in
the mid-eighteenth century as a 'hut' or summer residence for
Joseph Williamson, Advocate and Town Clerk. It certainly
appears on a number of eighteenth century maps, and in the
Ordnance Survey map of 1852 it is shown as a large villa with
a wing to the north and east, surrounded by a large
ornamental garden. In those days entry to it was from Sylvan
Place and also by way of a short lane opening from the east
side of Argyle Place, about opposite Argyle Park Villa. One
of the earliest recorded transactions on 15.8.1734 was a
Contract of Feu of $2\frac{1}{2}$ acres of ground lying between what is
now Argyle Place and Sylvan Place, between Sir James
Johnston of Westerhall and Hugh Fleming, Writer to the
Signet. By 1885, when the tenement buildings at Nos. 11 and
12 Sylvan Place were being built by Town & Country
Heritable Trust Ltd., part of the feu was described as
containing two old dwelling houses, the eastmost of which was
to be demolished and alterations made on the east gable of the
remaining house.

Today, hidden from view by the tenement buildings, Sylvan
House still exudes old-world charm from beneath a weight of
scaffolding and builders' equipment. Thanks to the foresight of
the present owner, the property is being skilfully restored in
keeping with its original appearance. The modern cement

render is being replaced with a lime harl, and internally many of the original features, including the staircase and the Baltic pine panelling, have been retained. Removal of the old cement render on the external walls has revealed that at some time in the past, the roof level has been raised to improve the attic accommodation. An interesting feature of the front of the building is the ornate door surround in sculptured stone, probably dating from the time when Sylvan House was a much larger property.

West St. Giles Church

Already there is in Edinburgh a generation of young people which has never known West St. Giles Church. Although the building and its elegant spire succumbed to the bulldozer some years ago, at least its cherished memory is never far from the thoughts of those members of its former congregation who now live at Argyle Park House built by the Viewpoint Housing Association on the site of the old church.

Of all the churches in the district, it has perhaps the most interesting history, having originated in 1699 in the Cathedral Church of St. Giles in the High Street. At that time it took the name New North Kirk under the leadership of its first minister, the Rev. George Andrews, and continued under that name with a succession of eminent clergymen for almost two hundred years. In 1829 the congregation moved out temporarily to allow so-called restoration work to be done to the Cathedral and, having lost its own place of worship, was required to make arrangements first at the Methodist Chapel in Nicolson Square and then at the Brighton St. Chapel. Not only did the congregation have the inconvenience of a somewhat nomadic existence but they suffered the additional setback in 1843 of seeing their minister, the Rev. C.J. Brown, join the Free Secession at the time of the Disruption. Undaunted, the congregation moved back into St. Giles, soon after taking the name West St. Giles.

Fig 55.   West St. Giles Church, looking west from Argyle Park Terrace.
Courtesy of the Royal Commission on the Ancient and Historical Monuments of Scotland

For the next few decades the congregation worshipped at St. Giles without serious incident, but by the late 1870s there was yet another change on the horizon. Dr. William Chambers had already done a great deal of restoration work at St. Giles with a view to opening up the entire Cathedral as one place of worship. Following a meeting of the Kirk Session on 21.5.1879, it was agreed that the congregation would move out, provided that a satisfactory arrangement could be made. With the assistance of a gift of £10,000, the congregation left St. Giles and found a home in the new and growing district of

Warrender Park. An old detached villa, Meadow Lodge, was acquired for £2,400, and the architects Hardy & Wight were commissioned to draw up plans for a new church which was completed in 1883. Until it was completed, services were held each Sunday in a temporary iron church which stood close to where Marchmont Road now meets Melville Drive.

The new West St. Giles Church was opened on 17.1.1883, separate services being taken by Professor Flint, Dr. Williamson and Dr. Mitchell before a capacity attendance. Over the years the church and its congregation grew in strength and influence until 1972, when it was decided that West St. Giles should form a union with Grange Church and Warrender Church. Sadly, the elegant building of West St. Giles in the Meadows was no longer required, and after standing empty for some time it was demolished to make way for the present flats. Fortunately some of the stained glass windows were saved and are now preserved in the new place of worship in Kilgraston Road under the name Marchmont St. Giles.

Argyle Place Church

Although Argyle Place Church cannot claim to rival the antiquity of West St. Giles Church, nevertheless Argyle Place Church had a most interesting origin.

In the 1870s the question of the use of unfermented wine at Communion began to be very acute, and a number of members had already left the Church on account of their strong objection to the practice. In an endeavour to find a solution to the problem within the denomination, a meeting was advertised of 'those favourable to the formation of a church in Edinburgh on temperance principles'. A meeting took place on 10.10.1876 and was followed by a public meeting on 24.10.1876 at which it was stated that 'while it was the distinct understanding only to use unfermented wine for Communion purposes total abstinence should not be made a

Fig 56.   Argyle Place Church, extensively damaged by fire in 1974.
Courtesy of Douglas F. Stewart

term of Communion'. History does not record if this 'escape clause' had any effect on the number of persons wishing to join the new congregation, but in May 1877 a petition was granted by the Presbytery for constitution as a congregation, and the first service was taken by the Rev. James Robertson Jun. on 13.5.1877.

The congregation having been established and substantial progress made in setting up the day-to-day organisation of the church, there remained the question of finding a permanent home for the new congregation. The young people of the church were in no doubt about the proposed site. At the foot of what is now Chalmers Crescent there was an old property called Lovers' Loan Cottage, standing in a garden which at one time had been an orchard. The property was on a short lease, and all around large-scale building operations were already under way. No doubt the enthusiastic congregation saw the tremendous potential in the new population. Eventually the site was secured, plans were prepared by the architect Alex

McTavish, and the memorial stone was laid on 1.11.1879 by Lord Provost William Collins of Glasgow. The church was opened on 27.5.1880, and the congregation settled down under its first minister, Rev. John Kay, to build up its reputation and influence in the new district of Warrender Park.

The church held its Jubilee Celebration on 1.5.1927. Two years later it became a parish church within the Church of Scotland as a result of the Union of 1929 which healed the breach caused by the Disruption in 1843.

In 1968 a Union was arranged between the Churches of Argyle Place and St. Catherine's in Grange, when it was decided to use Argyle Place Church as the future place of worship, with St. Catherine's in Grange as hall accommodation. Unfortunately, during renovations of Argyle Place Church in 1974, a serious fire broke out which caused extensive damage. It was eventually decided to demolish the remains of the fabric and to restore St. Catherine's in Grange for use as a place of worship.

The German-Speaking Church

On the other side of the street from the old Argyle Place Church is the Congregation of the German-Speaking Church, which has been in Chalmers Crescent since 1954. Devotees of the art of ballroom dancing, perhaps now with joints less supple, may remember the site as that of Glendinning's School of Dancing. When the dance school was discontinued in the 1950s, the German Church acquired the old villa as the manse, and converted the dance hall into a place of worship. They continued in the old premises until 1966, when a grand new church was built, under the supervision of Alan Reiach & Partners, Architects, to designs by the German architect Alfred Schilt of Frankfurt. The main feature of the church is the long stained glass window of modern, abstract design. The building, which includes a church, manse, hall and small library, undoubtedly serves as the social and religious centre of the

Fig 57. The German Church, designed by Alfred Schilt of Frankfurt, was opened in 1966.

Photograph by A.C. Robson

German community in Edinburgh and the East of Scotland.

These social and religious needs, however, existed in Edinburgh long before the congregation came to Chalmers Crescent. In the middle of the nineteenth century there was in Edinburgh a sufficient number of German-speaking people to form the nucleus of a congregation. With the assistance and encouragement of the United Presbyterian Church and the Church of Scotland, Johann Blumenreich secured the use of a hall in Upper Queen Street for the purpose of holding regular services in 1862. The hall was part of the United Presbyterian College, the site of which was very close to the present-day offices of the B.B.C., in Queen Street, and was used by the congregation until they built their own church in 1879 at the corner of Cornwallis Place and Rodney Street. At the outbreak of the First World War, as the congregation was unable to meet, it was disbanded and the church building was taken over by the Brethren. The congregation did not reconvene until the end of the Second World War, when

Fig 58.   Argyle Place, built on the site of Argyle Park Villa.
Photograph by A.C. Robson

accommodation was obtained on a temporary basis at St. Mary's Cathedral and Holy Trinity near Dean Bridge.

Thus, after a break of more than thirty years, the German Church has re-established itself, now in modern premises, and is still able to maintain its own special traditions. The service is a mixture of the rites of the Lutheran and Presbyterian Churches.

CHAPTER 9

The Meadows and Bruntsfield Links

Although there are many areas to the south of the Old Town which can claim some association with the Meadows and the Links, pride of place must surely go to the district of Marchmont, the northern and western boundaries of which look out over this large expanse of relatively unspoiled parkland. It is probably true to say that there are few areas in Edinburgh which have been more involved in the daily life and leisure of such a large concentration of the population. Being surrounded on all sides by residential and institutional development of almost every style and character, its continued existence, as a place of amenity for all, is constantly under attack. That amenity for one group is seen as wanton destruction by another group, is a dilemma which has beset the most even-handed of our civic leaders over several centuries. Whatever be the outcome of Lothian Region's experiment to allow a cycle track on Middle Meadow Walk, let the antagonists take note that in times past the civic authorities of the day considered, but refused, similar applications to allow the Walk to be used firstly as a carriageway for hackney coaches and then as a track for the very latest form of public tramways.

The East and West Meadows

The area of parkland on either side of Middle Meadow Walk, now known as the East Meadows and the West Meadows, was at one time the Burgh Loch or South Loch of the Old Town of Edinburgh. Named to distinguish it from the North Loch (which occupied the area now laid out as Princes Street Gardens and Waverley Station), the South Loch was for long one of the principal water supplies for the town, before the days of piped water from the springs at Comiston and Swanston. In terms of present day locations the loch was bounded, on the north, by the tree-lined avenue along the southern boundary of the Royal Infirmary, on the south by Melville Drive, on the east by Buccleuch Street, and on the west by the area around the stone pillars at Brougham Place. Although the loch was successfully drained many years ago, its name has been perpetuated in the picturesque street names of Lochrin at the west end and Borough Loch Lane at the east end.

The present day Meadows, however, with lush green grass, hard-surface paths and lines of elegant trees, do not give much indication of the character of the area and the use to which the loch was put in the early days. During the sixteenth century this expanse of water served a variety of needs, for the town in general, and for the people in the neighbouring houses, but the conflict between private amenity and the public good was ever present. Whilst it was undoubtedly convenient to use the water for washing clothes and watering horses, it was necessary for the authorities to introduce regulations from time to time to maintain a sufficient volume of clear water to supply the population of the Old Town. A dyke was built to keep the water in and to enable its escape route at Lochrin to be controlled at times of water shortage. Regulations of 1570 and 1581 were introduced to prevent breaches of the dyke 'to the hurt of the toun in this tyme of drowth', and at least one person was imprisoned for 'casting down the march dyke'. Even these precautions were not, however, entirely successful, because during periods of dry weather the water level dropped so low that murky pools and marshland were created along the whole length of the south bank. Tranquil it may have been: salubrious it certainly was not. No doubt conscious of the appalling lack of hygiene, the Scottish Parliament passed an Act in 1621 to bring in a gravitation supply of water from the springs at Comiston, but owing to a number of delays the scheme was not actually introduced until 1676.

Progress with draining the loch and improving the

Fig 59.   A lone figure on the banks of the Burgh Loch.

Engraving from Grant's Old & New Edinburgh

Fig 60.   Sheep grazing in the Meadows, 1910.

Courtesy of W.B. Grubb

surrounding area made but slow progress. After the decision in 1657 to drain the South Loch, the matter was put in the hands of John Straiton, who spent considerable effort and money on a number of schemes which were not entirely successful. Fortunately, however, entrepreneurs, keen to accept the civic challenge, were not in short supply, one of them being Thomas Hope of Rankeillour who in 1722 took over the task of draining the loch and laying out an ornamental park. Although Hope's involvement in the district was, like Straiton's, only partially successful, at least his efforts secured some degree of posterity in the street names of Hope Park nearby. In the opening years of the nineteenth century it was obvious to the Town Council that the draining of the loch was far from satisfactory and that it still presented a health hazard to the growing population on its south bank. A much more elaborate system of drainage was therefore built to draw off the natural water to the east through a covered drain into Holyrood Park.

With the problem of the drainage cured, or at least substantially improved, the Town was then able to concentrate on laying out the Meadows in a manner which would provide recreational amenities for the people. Several reports were considered, one of which, by Thomas Davies, won first prize in a competition sponsored by the Town, but which was bitterly attacked by Robert F. Gourlay in his own report of 1852. It was Gourlay who proposed in a report to His Royal Highness Prince Albert that most of the trees should be cut down and sold for 30/- each, the money received to be used to defray the expenses of a massive new road development across the Meadows. His contention was that as the Meadows had been abandoned by the population of the Old Town transferring to Craig's New Town, the area might as well be used in improving communication with the new suburbs growing up around the Grange. Pressure from the feuars of ground on the Dick–Lauder estates continued for some years until the idea was eventually quashed by the Kemp Report of 1873.

Fig 61.   High fliers at the Meadows Festival showground.
Photograph by A.C. Robson

In more modern times the Meadows has certainly been the home of many recreational and functional pursuits. Although the early proposals for curling, and for bleaching clothes, have not survived, archery, football, tennis, bowls and cricket are still very much in evidence. The Royal Company of Archers still shoot in the East Meadows, the Royal Highland Agricultural Show was held there in the early part of the present century, and nowadays there is the invigorating presence of the Meadows Festival, presented annually by a consortium of local organisations.

International Exhibition, 1886

There can be little doubt that the Meadows' finest hour was in 1886, at the time of the International Exhibition of Industry, Science and Art. The brainchild of architect and engineer James Gowans, it was the first International Exhibition ever brought to Scotland. Held on twenty-five acres of the West

Fig 62.   International Exhibition of Industry, Science & Art in the West Meadows, 1886.

Courtesy of Edinburgh City Libraries

Meadows during the entire summer and early autumn of 1886, it contained fifteen separate sections including Minerals, Pottery, Chemistry, Paper, Prime Movers, Railways, Tramways, Furniture and Educational Appliances. In a gesture which would be seen nowadays as nothing short of patronising effrontery, the organisers boasted of a section devoted to Women's Work (embroidery and needlework) and another given over to Artisans' Work, the latter intended 'to evoke and afford opportunity for display of the talent and ingenuity of the Working Classes'.

On the day that the Exhibition was opened by Prince Albert Victor, Edinburgh was in festive mood. The procession left the City Chambers to travel down the Mound, along Princes Street, up Lothian Road and into the Meadows from Brougham Place. The whole route and many of the surrounding streets were adorned with flags and balloons, except the General Post Office and Register House which retained their everyday appearance 'as befitted the chosen abodes of staid departments of the public service'. In striking contrast, however, Brougham Street was elaborately decorated with Venetian Masts surrounded by flags of different nationalities and hung with festoons and banners. At the grand entrance a crowd of 30,000 people awaited the arrival of the Prince.

The part played by James Gowans in the Exhibition was immense. Not only was he chairman of the Executive Committee, but he also made a valuable contribution in the shape of Model Dwelling Houses for ordinary people. He was one of the foremost architects of his day who believed that greater consideration should be given to the social aspects of house design, an idea which won for him the Diploma of Honour. His Model Dwelling Houses were erected in the north-east corner of the Exhibition grounds under the supervision of Thomas P. Marwick, an architect who had already been involved in the design of a number of tenements in Marchmont. All the very latest fittings and gadgets were included by suppliers keen to advertise their products. After all, in 1886 Marchmont was still being built, and to win a contract to supply baths or bells or railings was of considerable commercial value. There were Bower's Patent Regenerative Gas Lamps and Tobin's Ventilating Tubes — which probably augmented one another, although perhaps not intentionally. William Omit of High Riggs supplied malleable iron stair railings in a variety of designs, and William Scott Morton of Tynecastle was expert in fitting his own Patent Blower Slow Combustion Grate. Baths, of course, were very fashionable, especially those by Shanks & Co., japanned inside and out, with ornamental feet, and designed to stand without woodwork. And who more suited by name and reputation to put a good strong roof over the whole lot than Andrew Slater, the slater?

On 18th June Queen Victoria visited the Exhibition, an event which was marked by a Highland Gathering and a series of balloon ascents by Captain Dale in his gas-filled Sunbeam. Later that day the immense organisational ability of the Exhibition's prime mover was recognised, when James Gowans was knighted by Her Majesty. His active life had, however, taken its toll, and he died a few years later and was buried in Grange Cemetery.

Not only did the Exhibition bring immense prestige to the City during the year 1886, but there were also a number of

Fig 63.   The Prince Albert Sundial in the West Meadows.
Photograph by A.C. Robson

permanent acquisitions for the Meadows. The Prince Albert
Victor sundial still stands in the West Meadows, having been
erected to mark the opening of the Exhibition by His Royal
Highness. It is a most interesting octagonal pillar surmounted
by a bronze armillary sphere which acts as a sun dial. Eight of
the eleven courses of stone represent a different quarry with
various colours of stone. Starting from the bottom course these
are: Moat (red); Corncockle (red); Whitsome Newton
(yellow); Cragg (yellow); Myreton (blue); Cocklaw (yellow);
Redhall (yellow); Myreton (blue); Ballochmyle (red); Myreton

(blue); and Redhall (yellow). On the ninth course there are shields bearing the coronet of the Prince, the arms of the Marquess of Lothian, the cipher of the Lord Provost with the City Arms, and the Scottish Arms. The top plinth contains the words: 'Tak tent o' time, ere time be tint'.

Equally interesting are the Memorial Pillars erected by the Master Builders and Operative Masons of Edinburgh and Leith, at the west end of Melville Drive. The pillars are twenty-six feet high, consisting of eighteen courses of octagonal-shaped stone capped by massive blocks on which sit unicorns each seven feet high. As in the Prince Albert sundial, a number of quarries are represented, and in addition various kinds of masons' work are illustrated on the plain faces of the shaft, i.e. nidged, daubed, splitter striped and many more. The twenty-four shields display the Scottish, English and Irish Arms, the coats of arms of nineteen Scottish burghs, and the crest of the Edinburgh masons. Among the quarries represented are Dunmore and Prudham, from which large quantities of stone were taken for the construction of the tenement buildings of Marchmont.

The last, but no less interesting, memento of the Exhibition is the whale jawbone arch at the junction of the Jawbone Walk with Melville Drive, gifted to the City by the Zetland and Fair Isle Knitting stand.

Helen Acquroff Fountain

Close to the jawbone but not associated with the International Exhibition is a small fountain of polished marble, now bereft of the elixir of life but still clearly displaying the inscription

> In Memoriam: Helen Acquroff Sister Cathedral 1889 Erected by Members of I.O.G.T. & other friends

Helen Acquroff was a teacher of music for many years who built up a considerable reputation in the Edinburgh theatres and concert halls as a singer and a pianist. Because of her

Fig 64.   The Helen Acquroff Fountain, 1889.
Photograph by A.C. Robson

blindness, it was the custom for her to be escorted to these engagements by her niece, whose duty it was to inform her aunt of the names of the dignitaries present at the recital. Before the end of the evening's entertainment Helen had usually managed to put together one or two verses in recognition of the guest of honour, a practice which the audience came to expect as one of the highlights of the programme.

Offstage she was no less audible. An ardent and popular orator on temperance, she spent much of her time in the service of the Independent Order of Good Templars, for whom she wrote a short book entitled *Good Templar Songs & Readings*. She took the name Sister Cathedral from her great love of cathedrals, particularly St. Mary's Cathedral in Edinburgh.

Sadly, the fountain has again suffered damage by vandals in recent months.

Bruntsfield Links

On the south side of Melville Drive and extending up beyond
Whitehouse Loan is Bruntsfield Links, the last remnants of the
once famous Burgh Muir, one time popular hunting ground of
the Scottish nobility, and place of refuge for innumerable
outlaws and social outcasts. Now dissected by the roadway
leading from Barclay Terrace to Bruntsfield Hospital, it still
retains a number of interesting links with former times. In
contrast to the Meadows, which was developed out of the
marshland of the Burgh Loch, the Links was developed from
the harsh rocky terrain of the Town's early quarry holes.
Substantially reduced in size by the feuing of land around the
area now occupied by the tenement buildings of Tarvit Street
and the villas of Greenhill, the Links has been protected against
further encroachment by the Edinburgh Improvement Act of
1827 which prohibits the erection of buildings on the Links or
the Meadows. Like the Meadows, it has been the subject of
controversy over the years as to how best it can accommodate
demands as wide-ranging as the game of golf, the drying of
clothes, burying the dead, drawing water, mustering troops,
and digging for stones.

As early as 1599 there is recorded in the annals of the town
reference to the 'great stone quarries near to the lands of
Brownfield', and in 1694 the Town Council Minutes record
liberty to Patrick Carfrae, deacon of the masons, to quarry
stones in Bruntsfield Links. Again in the middle of the
eighteenth century Archibald Campbell, tacksman of
Bruntsfield Links, was given permission to make trial in the
City's quarries in the Links for stones for the New Charity
Workhouse, and in 1741 John Hog obtained a similar
concession to extract material for the rebuilding of tenements
at the Luckenbooths. An important proviso was inserted in
Hog's contract to prevent his working any part of the Links
used for the Citizens' Diversion and Recreation in the Golf.
That these quarries continued in existence for more than two
centuries is evidence that there was good-quality stone

available, even although it may not have been in vast quantities. Even as late as 1880, when Spottiswoode Street and Warrender Park Terrace were being built, these great stone quarries were still in existence and causing concern to the surveyors Carfrae and Belfrage when laying the public sewers and diverting the water pipes from Comiston and Swanston. One such quarry, lying at the foot of what is now Spottiswoode Street, near the boundary between the Links and the private ground of Sir George Warrender, was particularly troublesome because of its depth, and because it was partly filled with water. At a time when the tenement buildings were being erected all around, advertisements appeared in the Edinburgh newspapers of the day drawing attention to the 'free toom' at Warrender Park — forerunner no doubt of the municipal tips of the present day.

No activity on the Links, however practical in its application, ever took precedence over that most compelling of all Scottish pursuits, the game of golf. Lest anyone should be unaware of the rules and regulations of this most ancient of sports, listen to the words of the *Strangers' Guide to Edinburgh* for the year 1807:

> The balls used are extremely hard and about the size of a tennis ball(?) and the club with which the ball is struck is formed of ash, slender and elastic, having a crooked head faced with horn and loaded with lead to render it heavy. A set of clubs consists of five in number — a play club for giving the stroke, a scraper, a spoon, an iron headed club and a short club called a putter. The second, third and forth of these are used for removing the ball from inconvenient situations and the putter where a short stroke only is intended. The ball is struck by these clubs into small holes about $\frac{1}{4}$ mile distant from one another....

Golf's importance, and its ability to take precedence over matters of seemingly greater practicality, frequently dismayed and angered those who dared to cramp its style. In 1791, the first round was lost by the Parliamentary Trustees to the Council who had proposed securing part of the land used by the Burgess Golf Society in order to build a new road round the east side of Wrightshouses so as to avoid, in the words of one observer, 'so narrow and dirty a village, inhabited by so many low people'. A few years later, apparently undaunted by the precedent already set, Sir Walter Scott, as Secretary of the Royal Edinburgh Light Dragoons, made formal application to the Council for the occasional use of the Links for drilling, but after consulting the various Golfing Societies, the Council declined the application. Golf, to the exclusion of horses, was given further precedence in 1812 when certain overtures made by the Burgess Society were successful in preventing a local riding school called the Royal Manege from capitalising on the growing disregard for the 'no horses' rule.

The Golfing Societies, with their security of tenure so jealously guarded, were not however unmindful of their unique position, and during their long history did much to improve every aspect of the game. From the very earliest times the Links was the home of a number of important clubs, the most ancient of which was the Burgess Golf Society founded in 1735, forerunner of the Royal Burgess Golfing Society of Edinburgh. Another of the early clubs was the Bruntsfield, founded in 1761 (now the Bruntsfield Links Golfing Society at Davidson's Mains), followed in the nineteenth century by a host of smaller clubs, including the Allied in 1856 and the Warrender in 1858. Although Warrender may not have had the largest membership, it certainly gained considerable publicity from the able pen of James Ballantine, 'Poet Laureate of the West Port', who resided at Warrender Lodge when the Club was at the height of its popularity.

WARRENDER GOLF CLUB SONG
Air—'The Laird o' Cockpen'

Ye surely hae heard o' our Warrender Club?
It's time ye a' kenned about Warrender Club!
When a leal Scottish Bardie their Captain they dub,
He may weel sing the praises o' Warrender Club.

We're a' jolly fellows, wha baith tak an' gie
When our club's on the swing, and our ba's on the tee;
Afar! there, a-head, gin ye want na' a rub
Frae the sky-scraping ba's o' our Warrender Club.

Our hearts they are warm, and our breasts they are clean,
We come to seek pleasure and health on the green;
A' envy we banish, a' ill-will we snub,
Sic fiends daurna enter our Warrender Club.

We lo'e the green turf, and we lo'e the blue sky,
We lo'e every golfer wha aims far an' high;
We lo'e our wee drappie, we relish our grub
When sweetened by friendship in Warrender Club.

We hae stuffy wee chields for our Paterson paps,
For our long flyping strokes we hae long flyping chaps;
They maun be buirdly birkies wha ettle to drub
At putting or driving our Warrender Club.

Then, hip, hip, hurrah! for our Country and Queen,
And hip, hip, hurrah! for our Cock o' the green;
Gie traitors and cravens to auld Belzebub,
And hurrah! for the true men o' Warrender Club.

The popularity of golf does not, of course, derive solely from tramping across the turf. Every respectable course has its nineteenth hole, where even the most disastrous score can be seen in a different light. The Golf Tavern at Wright's Houses near the Barclay Church has for long been the popular retreat of those who, in the words of the poet Allan Ramsay, 'were weary'd at the gowff'. Believed to have been established in 1456, it still exists as the centre of golfing activity on the Links.

Another name closely associated with the early days of golf on the Links is that of Golfhall. As early as 1717 there is evidence that James Brownhill obtained a feu at the west end of the Links on which he built a house which was later used as a tavern under the name Golfhall. But the name has been used for more than one establishment in and around the Links. According to Boog Watson, that veritable storehouse of information relating to Edinburgh, Golfhall was also the name given to a house which stood at the east end of the Links on the ground which is now occupied by those tenement buildings of Meadow Place which face due west. Ainslie's Map of 1804 shows the ground owned by Mr. Martin, later occupied by J. Robertson the golfball maker and then by Warrender Golf Club.

Unlike the Meadows, which has a number of monumental plaques, shields and other ornamentations, the Links retains but one, the origin of which is already becoming obscure. At the highest, most exposed, and possibly the coldest spot on the Links there is a stone seat placed there at a time of civic pride but now blighted by the slogans of Edinburgh's gang warfare. The official inscriptions read:

1848 W D 1918 GRATITUDE IS A DUTY 1856 JHD 1924
1858 J G 1934 HE LIVED NEAR AND LOVED THESE
LINKS

L

CHAPTER 10

Transport; Traders; People

There are few subjects more likely to pander to nostalgia than the transport system of a bygone age, and Edinburgh, far from being an exception, is probably a leader in the field. Each succeeding generation has claimed that the horse-drawn bus, the horse-drawn tram, the steam-driven bus, the cable car and the electric tramway were, in their day, the acme of achievement in the world of civic transport. Nostalgia is not, of course, just a thing of the past! The young boys of today extol the virtues of Lothian Region Transport's latest electronic digital super-bus with the same enthusiasm as octogenarians recall how they emptied the sand box to help the horses to get a better grip in icy conditions. Despite the immense improvements in technology over the years, most of Edinburgh's transport eras have taken place during the lifetime of our oldest citizens, and the district of Marchmont has always featured prominently in most of the experiments.

Today it is possible to journey from the High Street to Marchmont by service number 41 in a few minutes for a fare of 20p, but in 1806 there was no service 41 and there were no families living in tenement buildings in Marchmont. However, in the little hamlet of New Campbeltown (now Roseneath) a new row of terraced houses had just been built, and Meadow Place was listed in the transport regulations of the day. For the sum of 2/- any citizen (apparently regardless of his weight) could be taken from the High Street to Meadow Place 'at the back of the Meadows' in a hackney chair, supported on horizontal poles, by two stalwart chairmen, in the style of the old sedan chair. How they coped with the soft ground round the badly drained South Loch is not recorded, but if the journey were attempted 'under cloud of night', the chairman was obliged to show a fixed light on the forepart of one of the poles. A further regulation, which would have placed an intolerable burden on any modern transport authority facing the problem of vandalism, enacted that if the lining or cushion of the chair was dirty or torn, a reduction of 1/- could be demanded in the fare. Although the hackney chair gradually disappeared from the Edinburgh streets in the early part of the nineteenth century, the hackney coach remained in vogue for very much longer, with horse-cab ranks in Warrender Park Road and Alvanley Terrace well into the twentieth century.

In 1870, when Sir George Warrender was occupying his mind with the question of feuing his estate at Warrender Park, horse-buses were operating a 'Morningside Circle' route along Grange Road, though the Magistrates had refused an application from Mr. A. Ritchie to run a steam bus between Waverley and Strathearn Road. Under the Edinburgh Tramways Act of 1871 the Edinburgh Street Tramways Company established a number of tramway routes, including one from Church Hill, via Clinton Road, Hope Terrace, Kilgraston Road and Grange Road, to Salisbury Place, but the Statute made it clear that the system was to be worked by animal power only. Despite the addition of trace horses on the steep hills and an average of only 5.8 miles per day for each animal, there were many complaints about the system, and allegations of cruelty to the livestock. Edinburgh, however, was loath to abandon the system, despite the fact that a steam tramway engine had performed well at a trial in 1881 and that an electric tram had been demonstrated at the International Exhibition in the Meadows in 1886. Transport and progress remained slow.

Following a study of the San Francisco cable-car system of the 1880s, the Edinburgh Northern Tramways Company was formed in 1884 to operate a cable-car service on the steep slopes on the north side of Princes Street, but it was not until 1893 that Edinburgh Corporation secured powers to convert the existing horse tramways in the town to cable operation. An Act of 1896 authorised a new route along Melville Drive and up Marchmont Road to connect with the Grange to

Salisbury route, but a suggested route to Warrender Park through Middle Meadow Walk was not taken up, despite an assurance that there would be automatic barriers to exclude other vehicular traffic. One of the two new power-houses to drive the underground cables was built at Tollcross in 1896–1899, and in the latter year the new tracks were laid in Strathearn Road and Place, avoiding the old route by Hope Terrace and Clinton Road. By then, many critics maintained that the Corporation was building a system which was already obsolete. Obsolete or not, the system demanded a great deal of skill from the driver to master the technique of gripping and releasing the running cable, especially at junctions where an auxiliary cable was introduced to enable the car to make a left- or right-hand turn at a reduced speed. Many of the complications at the junctions would have been avoided had it not been that the Bylaws prohibited any movement of cars by gravity, but in fact this had to be allowed eventually. Fortunately there was no similar prohibition against movement of the cars by horses, which were frequently relied upon to bring in stranded cars when a cable broke and brought that part of the system to a grinding halt.

No description of the cable-car system of Edinburgh would be complete without reference to its lighter side. There is no authentic account of drunk men being hauled home on a Saturday night with the end of their walking sticks jammed in the centre running cable, but it is beyond doubt that young boys were ever resourceful in putting the traction to unauthorised use. The simplest and visually most amusing trick was to tie a tin can to a piece of light string and to dangle the string in the slot on the roadway containing the moving cable, until the string was caught up, whereupon the tin can was pulled along the street like a miniature cable car until it met with an accident or fouled up the system.

Although electric trams were running in Musselburgh in 1904, Leith in 1905, and on a short line to Slateford in 1910, it was not until 1919 that Edinburgh decided on conversion to electric power. Implementation was delayed whilst the new

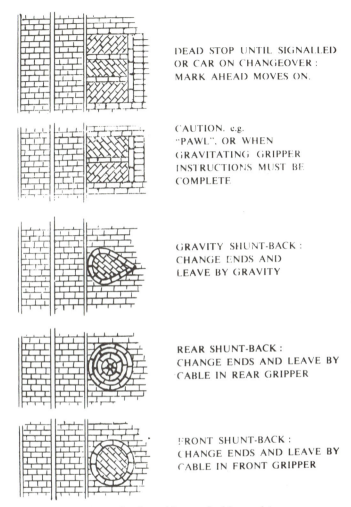

DEAD STOP UNTIL SIGNALLED
OR CAR ON CHANGEOVER :
MARK AHEAD MOVES ON.

CAUTION. e.g.
"PAWL", OR WHEN
GRAVITATING GRIPPER
INSTRUCTIONS MUST BE
COMPLETE

GRAVITY SHUNT-BACK :
CHANGE ENDS AND
LEAVE BY GRAVITY

REAR SHUNT-BACK :
CHANGE ENDS AND LEAVE BY
CABLE IN REAR GRIPPER

FRONT SHUNT-BACK :
CHANGE ENDS AND LEAVE BY
CABLE IN FRONT GRIPPER

Fig 65.   Road markings for the guidance of cable-car drivers.
Courtesy of D.L.G. Hunter

electric power station at Portobello was completed and sub-
stations equipped, but by 1922 the route to Nether Liberton
and along Grange Road to Church Hill had been provided
with poles and overhead lines. In the following year electric
power was installed on the West End to Marchmont Road

Fig 66.   Cable car at Marchmont Terminus, 1900
Courtesy of D.L.G. Hunter

line: service No. 6 with the identifying colour code of white
over red up beside the service number. After the junction at
the top of Marchmont Road had been relaid, it was possible in
1924 to introduce the familiar Marchmont Circle No. 6.

During the thirty odd years that the Marchmont Circle was
in existence the top of Marchmont Road was always the
centre of activity. It was here that the trams on the inner and
outer circle stopped to allow the driver and conductor time to

Fig 67.   Electric cars in Melville Drive in 1924.

Courtesy of D.L.G. Hunter. Photographed by the late E.O. Catford

Fig 68.   The Marchmont Circle No. 6 in Marchmont Road, 1956.

Courtesy of N.B. Traction Group Collection

have their piece and a flask of tea, contained in a metal box which looked strong enough to hold the Crown Jewels. There was a cross-over line used for a time by other services terminating there which was accompanied by the almost legendary changing over of the trolley and the reversing of all the seats. The trams themselves were very spacious, particularly at each end where the platform could hold a variety of luggage. Full coach-built prams were taken on without difficulty, creels of fish were commonplace in the days when Newhaven fishwives went on daily rounds, and even odd items of furniture were carried in do-it-yourself flittings. The trams were indeed versatile galleons, with a capability which extended to the most formal occasions. In 1952, when the bride and groom left West St. Giles Church by limousine to travel the short distance to the Grosvenor Hotel in Haymarket, the guests walked along to the bottom of Marchmont Road and boarded an Edinburgh Corporation tramcar en route for the reception. What perhaps some of them did not know was that the tram had to go via Grange Road, Salisbury, the Bridges, and Princes Street because the points at the foot of Lothian Road were incapable of allowing a tram to complete a left-hand turn towards Haymarket.

However, by the early 1950s many sections of track were in very poor condition, requiring huge sums of money for capital expenditure, and it was therefore decided to run down the system with a view to eventual closure. Over the following five years services were gradually taken over by buses, the tracks were lifted and the cobbles were replaced by tarmac. On 26.5.1956 the last tram ran on the Marchmont Circle, and on 16.11.1956 the last tram in Edinburgh ran from Braids via Bruntsfield, Tollcross and the Mound to Shrubhill depot, and thence to the breaker's yard.

Over the years the district of Marchmont has also been served by a number of bus services but, by and large, their success was usually confined to the years when the various tram systems were at their lowest ebb. In the 1890s, for example, when the conversion to cable cars was at its height, a

Fig 69. Edinburgh Corporation bus in 1914 on the Marchmont and Meadows route.

Courtesy of Lothian Region Transport

fifteen-minute bus service was introduced between the Mound and Warrender Park, and later a service was provided from Grange Loan, via Marchmont Road and Tollcross to Haymarket. In late 1906 the Edinburgh and District Motor Omnibus Company ran a circular route: Princes Street, Tollcross, Melville Drive, Marchmont Crescent, Sciennes Road, Salisbury and the Bridges, but the firm failed very soon afterwards. In 1914 Edinburgh Corporation started a circular bus service on the south side of the town to include Marchmont and the Meadows, but it was discontinued during the war years.

Traders

Long before the days of supermarkets and hypermarkets, generations of Scottish housewives 'got in their rations' without the use of the motor car, the shopping trolley or the credit card. Of course in those days there was much less to buy, and generally 'a forpit o' tatties' could be purchased at the local retail shop.

When Marchmont was built between 1876 and 1900, approximately 150 shop units were constructed, but the early feu-charters contained a number of restrictions, notably in connection with the sale of intoxicating liquor. Whilst the evils of alcohol were adequately guarded against, there was little or no control over the sale of unpasteurised milk, despite the fact that one-parent families seemed to be created at a greater rate by tuberculosis than by cirrhosis of the liver. In these 'romantic' days the corner-shop dairy was dependent for its daily supply on the arrival of the milk horse from one of the outlying farms near Edinburgh. When it arrived, the milk was emptied from one of the large urns into an open, shallow pan in the shop and then ladled into whatever receptacle the customer brought. And, of course, very few commodities were wrapped, packaged or bottled. Many of the customers arrived at the baker's shop with a beautifully laundered tea towel in which to wrap the day's bread freshly baked on the premises. The ovens and the bakehouse were built into the cellars below street level, and there was a large storehouse for the sacks of meal and flour. Just about everything came in large sacks: sugar, lentils, raisins, and even dog biscuits. A visit to a grocer then was a very different experience to a trip round a supermarket. This was the era of the cheese-wire, the butter scoop and the treacle jug. Tea was 1/6d a lb (7½p), and Van Houten's cocoa was a mere 6d a tin. There was Wigtownshire fresh cream, Loch Fyne kippered herrings and Duncan Flockhart's special Kola Water at 6d per bottle. A whole range of practical commodities were designed to ensure that even if a woman's work was never done, at least it would occupy her energy for the best part of the day: Nixey's black lead at 1d per cake; flue brushes for the chimney; carpet canes for the back green; Dolly Blue and Tints for wash-day blues; also Jujubes at 4d a quarter pound. Even the innuendo of the advertising world had a harsh reality about it: 'How to Please

Fig 70. John Horberry and his staff, 1901, at the shop in Warrender Park Road.

Courtesy of John Horberry & Son

a Husband! See that his Shirt Fronts and Collars are properly got up. If you find this is a difficult matter introduce your laundry-maid or washer woman to the St. Bernard's Enamel — simple and inexpensive to use'.

These early shopkeepers were not, however, without their pioneering spirit when it came to mechanisation. Shortly after St. Cuthbert's were established on the corner of Warrender Park Road and Marchmont Crescent, their dividend-hunters were regaled by a taste of real automation. Strung up on the beautiful plasterwork ceilings was a labyrinth of wheels, pulleys and shoots designed to ensure that cash transactions were completed with the minimum movement of staff. Communication between Miss Loraine, the shop manageress, and the cashier, marooned in a glass box, was maintained by inserting the cash into a large wooden ball and propelling it

Fig 71.   W.D. McGregor's shop, opened in 1907 at Strathearn Road.
Courtesy of the McGregor Family

the length of the shop, with a success rate largely dependent upon the effects of gravity, plus good luck.

The district was also served by a number of very competent tradesmen whose businesses are still there today. Although some of the work undertaken by the slaters and the joiners may not have altered very much over the years, by contrast the work of the electricians has changed completely. In fact, when the flats were first built electric power was not installed, open coal fires and town gas being the basic sources of power. When James Robb, the founder of James Robb (Electronics) Ltd., was building up his business, he spent a great deal of his time taking out the old gas pipes and brackets and installing electricity for the first time. Before everyone had electricity and mains radio sets, James Robb, and others like him, provided the essential service of re-charging the accumulators to power the old wireless sets.

Fig 72. Original frontage of Cuthill the butcher, established in 1892 in Warrender Park Road.

Photograph by Malcolm Liddle

The newsagents' shops were also owned and managed by a group of men whose interests and abilities extended well beyond the confines of their retail livelihood. In Marchmont Road there was Hugh Shaw, Manager of the Hibernian Football Club, and Callum MacDonald, who printed in his basement the works of famous Scottish poets, and in Marchmont Crescent John Robson built up a successful business after his return from India, in addition to being Sports Reporter for the *Edinburgh Evening Dispatch*.

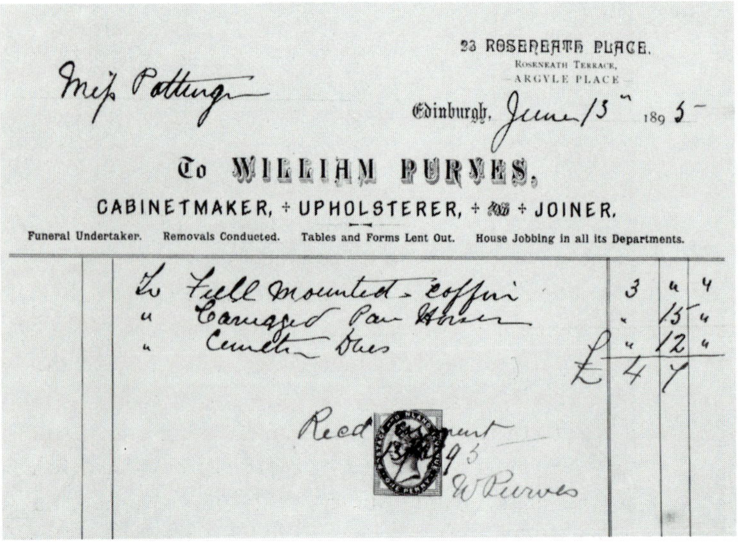

23 ROSENEATH PLACE.
ROSENEATH TERRACE,
ARGYLE PLACE

Miss Pottinger

Edinburgh, June 13th 1895

To WILLIAM PURVES,
CABINETMAKER, + UPHOLSTERER, + & + JOINER.
Funeral Undertaker. Removals Conducted. Tables and Forms Lent Out. House Jobbing in all its Departments.

To Full mounted coffin	3	"	4
" Carriage Pair Horses	"	15	"
" Cemetery Dues	"	12	"
	£ 4	7	

Recd payment 13 Jun 95
W Purves

Fig 73. In 1895 funerals were by carriage and horses.
Courtesy of John R. Purves

No study of the Marchmont business population would be complete without reference to the Purves family. As early as 1881 John Innes commenced business at 22 Argyle Place as an upholsterer and joiner, later moving with his partner Mr. Boyd to larger premises built in the garden ground of Westerhall Villa. By 1889 the business had been taken over by William Purves and extended to include that of funeral undertakers. When Westerhall was demolished by Turner the builder in 1896, William Purves moved out to 5 Meadow Place, which was the centre of the business for many years. In more recent years there were premises in Marchmont Road, and at the present time the business at Roseneath Street is in the fourth generation of the Purves family.

Population

By 1881 large sections of Marchmont had been completed, and

families were beginning to move in and to build up a community in an area of the town which, hitherto, had been open farmland. Edward Calvert had made a fine job of his elevations for Warrender Park Terrace, and W. & D. McGregor had completed their development at the extreme west side of the estate. Some isolated feus had not yet been built on, but, by and large, the older part of Marchmont was near completion.

The new population had no doubt displaced a small rural community which had worked the land of the North Park and the South Park for generations before, and in earlier days there had been a thriving industry in the numerous stone quarries. There were, of course, traces of the older community still to be seen. Just beyond the eastern boundary of Sir George's land there was the ancient community centred on what is now known as Roseneath and Argyle, and the boundary wall still separated the Lands of Bruntisfield from the hamlet of New Campbeltown. It was here that a number of artists and successful merchants in the City had established their country houses in earlier years, but the seclusion and tranquillity of the district was being threatened by large-scale tenement development.

At the west side of the estate the area once known as Brown's Acres was also under threat from the encroaching tenements. Viewpark had already lost a large section of its garden ground to allow the building of Warrender Park Crescent, but at least the old mansionhouse had been saved and was being used as Viewpark School. On a small triangular piece of ground at the east end of Warrender Park Crescent there was a successful market garden owned by David McKay, and at the west end Viewpark Cottage, not yet the home of Andrew Swan Watson, was occupied by a master plumber, his wife, domestic staff, nurse, and ten children.

The most significant link with the old community was, of course, Bruntsfield House which was still occupied by Sir George Warrender, his family and domestic staff, representing in all about thirty people. Judging by the description of the duties undertaken by the domestic staff, it would appear that in 1881 lines of demarcation and the 'Upstairs, Downstairs' approach to domestic service were still very much the accepted daily routine. The Warrender household consisted of Sir George, his son Hugh and his three daughters Margaret, Alice and Eleanor, with a complement of twelve domestic staff at the 'big hoose' itself. There was a cook and housekeeper, two ladies' maids, an upper laundrymaid, and an under laundrymaid. Then there was a kitchenmaid assisted by the scullery maid, an upper housemaid and an under housemaid. Thomas Ansell was the butler and Charles Johnstone and William Hasker were the footmen. In the little lodge at the Whitehouse Loan main gate resided Mr. and Mrs. King and their five children, Mr. King being the head gardener for the estate for many years. At the north-west corner of the estate grounds there was the stable lodge occupied by David Russell the coachman with his wife and son and daughter, and in a small bothy nearby there was William Harkess the groom.

Such, then, was the domestic staff at Bruntsfield House about a century ago. In those days, of course, it was not just the mansionhouses which had domestic staff. The larger of the Marchmont flats were constructed with accommodation for servants, usually consisting of a small room or curtained recess just off the kitchen. There was a system of service bells installed, with the bell-board in the kitchen where the servant could see which part of the house the summons came from. The bell was operated from the principal rooms of the house by 'cawing the handle' of a small black fitting positioned for convenience on either side of the fireplace. Although the master would not be sitting watching television, no doubt his calls for more coal or more fresh air would, in some households, constitute a significant part of the servant's daily routine. Life for someone in service was not, of course, all that easy, particularly in situations where there was also a basic difference in religion and outlook. At the end of the First World War, when the practice of having domestic servants was beginning to decline, there lived on the fringe of

Marchmont in Millerfield Place the Edinburgh Hebrew Congregation Rabbi, father of two of Edinburgh's most renowned members of the Daiches family. When Professor David Daiches recalls his childhood days around Marchmont, he refers to the difficulties experienced by his mother in training a Scottish maid to work in a rabbinical household. It was necessary to explain the different dishes for meat and milk, the importance of using different dishcloths for milchig and fleischig dishes, and of course the special arrangements for the Sabbath and for the many festivals.

It is interesting now to reflect upon the changed social pattern, particularly when it is remembered that in those days wives did not normally have salaried employment. When Warrender Park Road was built, cooks and servants were employed by people who held such occupations as seedsmen or secretaries, and in Marchmont Street the apparent luxury of domestic staff was by no means beyond the financial resources of a bank clerk or a law clerk.

Whatever these financial resources may have been, they were infinitely better than those of the small band of street musicians and characters who frequented Marchmont in those early days. 'Nightingale', with a voice fading fast from its former glory, was heard in the evenings to warble up and down the scale with a clarity which did not match that of her feathered rival in Berkeley Square. Of 'Bird's Nest' little is known except that frequently she was seen to huddle her mortal bones in a sheltered position in the Meadows with little to identify her, save the very distinctive hair style from which the nick-name was derived. Even as late as the early 1950s, before the chimney stacks began to crumble under the weight of pre-Coronation television aerials, the highlight of the evening's entertainment was undoubtedly that of Codona's one-man band. A lean, somewhat distant character, clearly in a class of his own, he was capable of producing a sound from his whistle and drum which could reach even the most reluctant of audiences, wherever they chose to be. At the bottom end of the scale, both social and melodic, was that class of entertainer least likely to have been influenced by the concept of Equity — legal, moral or theatrical — the back-green singer. Although some had a reasonable repertoire, for the most part they were shabby nameless itinerants with no voice and no future, possessed of a blend of politeness which was tempered by the accuracy of the aim and the value of the coin, tossed from a top-flat kitchen window. A threepenny piece, tightly wrapped in newspaper, would buy a pie in the morning and hopefully silence for the rest of the evening.

A feature of the population of Marchmont in its early years was the practice of architects and builders occupying houses which they had either designed or helped to build. The architect Edward Calvert lived for a while in a house which he had designed at No. 8 Warrender Park Terrace, Thomas P. Marwick the architect lived at 1 Spottiswoode Street, and Hippolyte Blanc lived at Thirlestane Road before moving to the grand house now occupied by the Iona Hotel. The builders, too, were sufficiently impressed by their own work to take up residence in Marchmont and presumably be answerable to their neighbours for any defects in the property. They frequently occupied the main-door flats and were not averse to indulging in the disproportionate allocation of feu duties, a practice which although perfectly legal was seen by other families as morally reprehensible.

The presence of so many families meant, of course, that the streets were always populated by a great number of children, despite the nearness of the Meadows. Unhappily for parents, the cobbled streets of Marchmont always seemed more attractive to children than the safety of the Meadows. Who, after all, could display all the refinements of bools or chuckies on the lush green grass of the old Burgh Loch, and who would partake of unnecessary exercise in Tumblers' Hollow in preference to whacking an iron gird down the echoing lanes off Roseneath Terrace? The almost complete absence of motorised transport created in most streets an arena capable of staging most of the junior 'Olympics' of the day. As late as 1950 streets like Marchmont Crescent were devoid of parked

Fig 74.   Miniature gardens grow to profusion on gracious top-flat landings.
Photograph by Trevor E.R. Yerbury

cars, and the greatest vehicular threat to children's safety came at a speed not greater than Leckie's Slow Burning Brickettes. Street games were still a major source of amusement, for boys and girls, right up to the age when the glissando of the wolf-whistle was received less contemptuously than before. There was Cockie-Leekie, Whitehorse and You Can't Cross the River, to say nothing of Giant Steps and Little Steps in which progression of the participants was regulated by a language of its own: take an umbrella; take a hot water bottle; a spitting kettle; a banana slide or a scissors! Whilst the boys were known, on occasion, to join in these games, they much preferred the rough and tumble of Bulldog or Collie-Buckie.

The games which were essentially for the fairer sex were peevers and skipping, both of which produced a science of their own. No self-respecting boy, wishing to avoid being called a 'feardie-gowk', would ever pass by a game of peever-beds without kicking the peever towards the nearest siver in the muted hope that it would plop down and be lost for ever. Skipping games were lengthy and imaginative, and always to the rhythm of one or other of the many rhymes reflecting every aspect of life:

> PK chewing gum
> Penny a packet
> First you chew
> Then you crack it
> Then you stick it
> In your jacket . . .

These games, and many more, were often regulated by an essentially practical concept worked out over the years by generations of children of different ages. In order to maintain strict impartiality and to minimise the risk of someone going off in the huff, each game was preceded by the legendary ritual 'one potato, two potato, three potato four . . .' to determine who was to be 'het' or 'out'. Such were the pleasures of the day.

No study of Marchmont's population would be complete without reference to the student population. Being within walking distance of the older Faculties of Edinburgh University, the Royal Infirmary and New College, Marchmont was ideally suited to house the growing population of students before the days of halls of residence. It was the realm of the student's landlady, even from the very earliest days. Many of the old photographs of Marchmont which survive to this day have been taken from actual postcards written by students in digs, and addressed to their families and friends in every part of the globe. Written many years ago by anxious adolescents, their thoughts and aspirations are essentially timeless: 'Have been terribly busy and got nothing done'; 'Arrived safely — don't know when I'll get a

Fig 75.   Orcadian poet and writer George Mackay Brown.
Photograph by Gunnie Moberg

night out'; 'Jim and I sail on the 9th'. By 1925 the Marchmont district had a separate entry in the Corporation Tramways Department publication of Apartments in the City of Edinburgh, with approximately 150 entries offering board and lodgings with or without attendance, at very moderate terms. Many of those students have now made their way in life but still recall with obvious pleasure those early days under the watchful eye of a Marchmont landlady. An early call for a good cooked breakfast, followed by a saunter across the Middle Meadow Walk for classes, and back in the evening for a three-course meal, seemed, in the 1950s, to be reasonable value at £3. 2/6d per week. The memory of those nostalgic years, of seemingly limitless freedom, has found expression in the works of at least two of Marchmont's literary giants, firstly in *The Golden Lamp* by Alasdair Alpin MacGregor and, in more recent years, in George Mackay Brown's novel *Greenvoe*.

Judging nowadays by the huge exodus of budding intellectuals from Marchmont every morning across the Middle Meadow Walk and the Jaw Bone Walk, it is a fair assumption that the district is still the home of many students, but many of the traditional landladies have gone from behind their net curtains. The warm Edinburgh welcome 'No Hawkers: No Circulars', at one time so discreetly displayed on every second door, has given way in certain areas to a variety of signs, one of which, 'No Admittance on Account of Foot and Mouth Disease', seems to convey more relaxed attitudes. Today, Edinburgh's middle class has become Marchmont's absentee landlords, purchasing flats as property investment and letting them to groups of young students. It is a practice which, with toleration and control, can be absorbed into the district without harm, but there is a body of local opinion which is against the trend making further inroads into a district which has always had a good balance of population.

Marchmont is not, however, just a students' dormitory. The present population, in approximately 2,500 high-value flats and other houses, is varied in age and occupation, and it would be quite wrong to give the impression that the entire area has a transient population. Indeed longevity and permanence seem to be a feature of the district. Examples of families and single people living in the same house for upwards of seventy years are common, and in one case which must be close to a record, an elderly resident has lived in Marchmont since 1893. She remembers Westerhall at Roseneath, she visited the Murrays at St. Margaret's Tower long before the acrimonious litigation of

Fig 76.   Mrs. Gillies, born in 1889, has lived in Marchmont since 1893.
Courtesy of G.M. Gillies

1904, and she recounts with lingering trepidation the first headmaster at Warrender Park Board School. Fortunately everyone does not have a memory like Mrs. Gillies, otherwise there would be little demand for a book on the history of Marchmont in Edinburgh.

SUGGESTIONS FOR FURTHER READING

Ballingall, William	*Edinburgh Past and Present*	1877
Book of the Old		
Edinburgh Club	esp. Vol. X	
Brown, George Mackay	*Greenvoe*	1975
City Architect's	*Catalogue of Monuments*	
Department	*and Burial Grounds*	
Couper, Rev. David	in *Disruption Worthies*	1876
Daiches, David	*Two Worlds*	1956
Downie, Hay	*Fifty Years at*	
	'Argyle Place', 1927–1977	1977
Edinburgh Exhibition	Edinburgh Room, Edinburgh	
Views and Notices, 1886	Central Public Library	1886
Edwards, Owen Dudley	*The Quest for Sherlock Holmes*	1983
Gibson, Thomas	*Argyle Place United Free*	
	Church, Edinburgh, 1877–1927	1927
Gladstone, J.W.E.	*Warrender Church, 1886–1936*	1936
Grange Association	*The Grange — A Case for*	
	Conservation	1982
Grant, James	*Old and New Edinburgh*	1882
Gray, John G.	*The South Side Story*	1962
Harrison, Wilmot	*Memorable Edinburgh Houses*	1971
Hunter, Alexander, M.D.	*Edina's International*	
	Exhibition	1886
Hunter, D.L.G.	*Edinburgh's Transport*	1964
Lawson, J.P.	*Hostels for Hikers, 1931–1981*	1981
Lee, Miss C. Fraser	*The Real St. Trinneans*	1962
McAra, Duncan	*Sir James Gowans:*	
	Romantic Rationalist	1975
MacGregor, Alasdair		
Alpin	*Auld Reekie*	1943
MacGregor, Alasdair		
Alpin	*The Golden Lamp*	1964
MacGregor, Alasdair		
Alpin	*The Turbulent Years*	1945
Maclean, Dr. Una	*The Usher Institute and the*	
	Evolution of Community	
	Medicine in Edinburgh	1975
McWilliam, Colin	*Scottish Townscape*	1975
Maxwell, Thomas	*St. Catherine's in*	
	Grange Church, 1866–1966	1966
Pringle, James	*Story of West St. Giles*	
	Church, 1699–1916	1916
Ritchie, James T.R.	*Golden City*	1965
Ritchie, James T.R.	*The Singing Street*	1964
St. Margaret's Convent,		
History of		1886
Searle, Ronald	*The St. Trinian's Story*	1959
Smith, Charles J.	*Historic South Edinburgh,*	1978
	2 vols.	1979
Warrender, Margaret	*Marchmont and the Humes*	
	of Polwarth	1894
Warrender, Margaret	*Walks near Edinburgh*	1895
Wilson, Sir Daniel	*Memorials of Edinburgh in*	
	the Olden Time	1891

Index

Acquroff Fountain 143
Adam, Patrick W., RSA 123, 124
Airlee Lodge 61
Alison, Prof. Wm. P. 46
Alvanley, Family name 15, 17
Alvanley Street 9, 63
Alvanley Terrace 7, 9, 39, 63, 66, 72
Anderson, J. & F., Solicitors 3
Arden, Family name 15, 17
Arden Street 9, 63, 64
Argyle Building Co. 118
Argyle Park House 120, 128
Argyle Park Terrace 118–120
Argyle Park Villa 17, 89, 116, 120, 127
Argyle Place 89, 115, 116, 127
Argyle Place Church 108, 130–32
Argyll, Duke of 17
Armour, Harry 59
Articles and Conditions of feu 6, 7
Ashfield 59

Ballantine, James 120, 147
Barclay Free Church 49, 102
Beacon Newspaper 116, 118
Beaufort Road 33, 100
Blaikie, Rev. Wm. G. 85, 112
Blanc, Hippolyte, Architect 9, 32, 166
Bonar, Rev. Horatius 101, 106
Boog-Watson, Charles 17, 148
Borough Loch (see also Burgh
   loch) 114
Boroughmuir School 41, 42, 81
Boswell, Sir Alex 118
Boswell, James 126
Bott's Swotts 48
Bowie, John 34
Broune, Richard 75
Brown, George Mackay 170
Brown's Acres 38, 163
Brownisfield Building Association 46
Bruntfield, Stephen 75
Bruntisfield, Lands of 1, 15, 62, 163
Bruntisfield, Lord 75
Bruntisfield Park statements of rent 7
Bruntisfield Road 3, 6, 31, 44
Bruntsfield Crescent 74
Bruntsfield Hospital 82–84
Bruntsfield House 1, 9, 15, 70, 75–79,
   164

Bruntsfield Links 7, 38, 66, 86, 135,
   145–49
Bruntsfield Links Golfing Society 147
Bruntsfield Links Hotel 7
Bruntsfield Links Memorial Stone
   Seat 149
Bruntsfield Park Hotel 7
Bryce, David, Architect 3, 20, 34, 39,
   51, 63, 72, 78
Budge, John 26
Burgess Golf Society 146
Burgh Loch (see also Borough
   loch) 135, 145, 166
Burgh Muir 75, 78, 88, 145

Calvert, Edward, Architect 9, 31, 35
Cameron, R. Macfarlane, Architect 85
Cant, Henry 77
Carfrae & Co., Surveyors 3, 7, 146
Carlung Place 112
Carved panels, table of dates and
   initials 14, 15
Chalmers Crescent 21, 104
Chalmers Memorial Free Church 106
Chambers, Dr. William 129
Christie, Alex, RSA 121
Christie, John 26
Clapperton, Margaret 88
Clinton Road 92, 151, 152
Court of Session 11, 96
Crowe, Thomas 31, 58
Cruikshank, G. 9, 64–66
Cruikshank, W.S. 9, 41, 64–67
Currie, Rev. Thomas 50, 84, 85

Daiches, Prof. David 62, 165
Davidson & Chisholm 9, 65
Dean of Guild Court 11, 41, 66, 67, 95,
   118, 123
Dick-Lauder family 103
Dick-Lauder, Sir Thomas 103
Doyle, Sir Arthur Conan 119, 120
Dunbar, W.T. & Sons 59, 94

Edinburgh Hebrew Congregation
   Rabbi 165
Edinburgh Improvement Act, 1827 145
Edinburgh Southern Cemetery
   Company 103

Edinburgh Tramways Act, 1871   151
Edwards, Owen Dudley   119
Exhibition of architectural drawings in
   Edinburgh, 1881   91

Fairlie, John   77
Fleming, Sir Alex   35
Flodden Lodge   59
Foot, Victorine   124
Fothergill, Dr Alan   72, 73

Gala House   111
Galloway & Mackintosh   9, 22, 31, 46
German Church   132–34
Gillespie Crescent   80, 81
Gillespie, James   80
Mrs Gillies   171
Gillis, Rev. James   88, 89, 91, 95, 98
Glendinning's School of Dancing   132
Golfhall   148
Golf Tavern   148
Gorgie & Dalry Housing Association   60
Gowans, Sir James   139, 141
Graham, James Gillespie   89
Grange Association   92
Grange Cemetery   102–106, 141
Grange House   77, 103
Grange Parish Church   86, 100, 102, 130
Grange Road   92, 103, 151
Gray, Cardinal Gordon   87
Greenhill   59
Greenhill Cottage   52, 72

Hackney chair   150
Hardy & Wight, Architects   130
Hay, John C., Architect   9, 33
Henderson, Simon   34
Hibernian Football Club   161
Holmes, Sherlock   119
Hope Terrace   92, 94, 151, 152
Hope, Thomas   138
House of Lords   11, 96, 120

Independent Order of Good
   Templars   144
International Exhibition of Industry,
   Science and Art, 1886   139–43, 151
Iona Hotel   92
Iron Church (Robertson Memorial)   100
Iron Church (Warrender Park)   50, 64,
   85
Iron Church (West St. Giles)   130
Irving, David, LLD   122

James Gillespie's Boys' School   21,
   24–29, 82
James Gillespie's High School   71, 79
James Gillespie's High School for
   Girls   28, 43, 82
James Gillespie's Hospital   43, 80
Jawbone Walk   143, 170
Jex-Blake, Dr. Sophia   83, 84
John Paul, Pope   87
Johnson, Dr. Samuel   126

Kay, Rev. John   132
Kilgraston Road   92, 100, 105
'Kippers & Pianos'   33
Kwik-Fit-Euro Ltd.   94

Landladies   168
Lauderdale, Family name   15, 17
Lauderdale Street   49, 63, 71, 79, 84
Lawdre, Alan de   75
Lee, Miss C. Fraser   109–111
Linlithgow & Stirlingshire Hunt   59
Littlejohn, Henry   47
Livingston, John   59
Lovers' Loan Cottage   131

McDonald, Right Hon. Andrew, Lord
   Provost   60
MacGregor, Alasdair Alpin   170
McGregor, W. & D.   9, 44, 66
McLaren, Duncan Jnr.   60
Macnaughten, Alex, Architect   31
Marchmont Building Association   46
Marchmont Circle   154, 156
Marchmont Crescent   3, 6, 20–24,
   116, 166
Marchmont Crescent South   22, 24
Marchmont, Family name   15, 17
Marchmont Garage   59
Marchmont Road   3, 20, 29–33, 151
Marchmont St. Giles Church   86,
   100–102, 130
Marchmont Street   3, 6
Marchmont Terrace   7, 9, 63, 72
Marwick, T.P., Architect   22, 35, 85,
   141, 166
Master Builders & Operative Masons of
   Edinburgh and Leith   143
Meadow Lodge   130
Meadow Place   116, 122, 123
Meadows   114, 135–39
Meadows Festival   139
Melville Drive   44, 114, 151

Menzies, John of Pitfodels 88
Middle Meadow Walk 104, 135, 152, 170
Morelands 58
Morham, Robert, Architect 100
Morningside Circle Horse Bus 151
Mount Grange 94, 95
Murray, David 95
Mutual Building Association 46

New Campbeltown 122–27, 150
Nisbet, John 34
North Park 3, 8, 36, 63, 163

Oliver, John 121, 123

Palmerston Building Association 33
Palmerston Road 104, 109, 111, 112
Park Road Building Association 46
Pasteur, Louis 47
'Pianos & Kippers' 33
Population 162–171
Prince Albert Victor sundial 142, 143
Pugin, Welby, Architect 91
Purves, Wm. 121, 162
Pyper, John 9, 22

Quarries:
    Blaxter 62
    Denwick 62
    Dunmore 6, 143
    generally 11, 13, 145
    Prudham 143
    Redhall 6
    South Park 66–68

Ramsay, Allan 148
Reiach, Alan, Architect 124
Reiach, Alan & Partners, Architects 132
Reid Memorial Church 102
Riach, Rev. W.L. 100
Rig, John 70
Robertson Memorial Church 100, 106
Romanes Family Trust 58
Roseneath 17
Roseneath Place 20, 115, 121
Roseneath Street 115, 120, 121
Roseneath Terrace 115, 121, 123, 166
Rowand Anderson, Kininmonth & Paul 79, 82
Royal Bank of Scotland 61, 99, 100
Royal Burgess Golfing Society of Edinburgh 147

Royal Company of Archers 139
Royal Edinburgh Light Dragoons 147
Royal Highland & Agricultural Society of Scotland 36, 139
Royal Society for the Prevention of Cruelty to Children 113

St. Ann's Villa/Seminary 90, 97–100
St. Bennet's 87, 92
St. Catherine's Argyle Church 106–108, 132
St. Giles Cathedral 128
St. Gillie Grange Building Association 46
St. Margaret's Cathedral 91
St. Margaret's Convent 43, 52, 87–91, 98, 104
St. Margaret's Tower 95–97, 170
St. Mary's Cathedral 144
St. Trinians, Belles of 109
St. Trinnean's School 109–111
Salvesen, Lord 72
Schilsky, Eric 124
Schilt, Alfred, Architect 132
Scott, Sir Walter 117, 121, 147
Scottish Youth Hostels Association 72–74
Searle, Ronald 109
Seftor, Arnold, Ltd. 22
Sentinel Newspaper 118
Shaw, Hugh 161
Shiells, R. Thornton, Architect 24
Sim, Alastair 109
Smeaton, Rev. Prof. 106
Souden, John 9, 33, 65
South Loch 114, 135, 138, 150
South Park 8, 62–66, 70
Spottiswoode, Family name 15, 17
Spottiswoode Road 9, 65, 68
Spottiswoode Street 62, 146
Spottiswoode Terrace 63
Stables 6, 57–61
Stevenson, Duncan, of the *Beacon* 116, 117
Stirling-Maxwell House 35
Straiton, John 138
Strathearn 17, 92
Strathearn Building Company 33
Strathearn College 93
Strathearn Place 87, 93, 152
Strathearn Road 92–95, 151
Strathfillan Road 93, 96
Street characters 165

Street games   167
Street musicians   165
Stuart, James of Dunearn   117, 118
Student magazine   34
Student population   168–70
Swann, John Russel   7, 8
Sylvan House   127, 128
Sylvan Place   127

Thirlestane, Family name   15, 17
Thirlestane Lane   31, 57–61
Thirlestane Lane Association   57
Thirlestane Road   43, 51–54, 91
Traders   157–62
Trail, Agnes   88
Trams, cable   151–53
Trams, electric   152–56
Trams, horse-drawn   151
Tumblers' Hollow   166

Ursulines of Jesus
see St. Margaret's Convent
Usher Hall   41
Usher Institute   46–48, 68

Viewpark   38, 39, 41, 163
Viewpark Cottage   43, 82
Viewpark School   41, 49, 163
Viewpoint Housing Association   128

Warrender Baths   54–57
Warrender Baths Club   54–57
Warrender Church   84–87, 102, 130
Warrender, Sir George 78, 85, 89, 146,
    151, 163
Warrender Golf Club   147, 149
Warrender Golf Club Song   147

Warrender Lodge   120, 121, 147
Warrender, Margaret   68, 70
Warrender Park   20, 34, 54, 75, 130
Warrender Park Board School   24–28,
    82, 171
Warrender Park Crescent   39, 66, 75, 82,
    163
Warrender Park Free Church   48–50
Warrender Park Road   44–46, 79, 84,
    116
Warrender Park Terrace   6, 34–36
Warrender Terrace   34
Warrender Tombstone   68–71, 79
Warrender, Sir Victor   78
Warrender's Lane   121
Water supply from Swanston,
    Comiston   54, 136
Watherston Feuing Plan, 1876–77   7–9,
    21, 31, 51
Watson, Andrew Swan,
    Photographer   39, 43, 82, 163
West St. Giles Church   102, 128–130,
    156
Westerhall   115–122
Westerhall Cottage   121
Westerhall Lodge   121
Westerhall Villa   121, 122, 162
Whitehouse Estate   17, 72, 93
Whitehouse Loan   52, 72, 79, 85, 88
Whitehouse Tennis Club   55, 93
Wilkie, David   57
William's Hut   127
Wilson, George Alex   95
Wilson, Robert, Architect   24
Wrychtishousis, Mansion of   80

Yew Tree House   121, 123